Who Am I, Really?

To Shirley,
Best Wishes,
Diane Koven
Nov. 2014

Who Am I, Really?

Adoption Stories

DIANE KOVEN

GSPH

GENERAL STORE PUBLISHING HOUSE INC.
499 O'Brien Road, Renfrew, Ontario, Canada K7V 4A6
Telephone 1.613.432.7697 or 1.800.465.6072
www.gsph.com

ISBN 978-1-77123-017-9

Copyright © Diane Koven 2013

Cover art, design, formatting: Magdalene Carson
Printed by Image Digital Printing Ltd.
dba The IDP Group, Renfrew, Ontario
Printed and bound in Canada

No part of this book may be reproduced, stored in a retrieval system,
or transmitted in any form or by any means without
the prior written permission of the publisher or,
in case of photocopying or other reprographic copying, a licence from
Access Copyright (Canadian Copyright Licensing Agency),
1 Yonge Street, Suite 1900, Toronto, Ontario, M5E 1E5.

Cataloguing data available at Library and Archives Canada

I dedicate this book to my children, Jeremy and Zahava, the best children any mother could ever hope for

And to the memory of my father, Jerry Koven, who believed that I could do anything.

Contents

ACKNOWLEDGEMENTS	*ix*
INTRODUCTION	*1*
David Sparks: *Redemption*	*5*
David's Story	*6*
Tim Groniger: *I love my moms*	*11*
Tim's Story	*12*
Thanh Campbell: *An orphan no longer*	*17*
Thanh's Story	*18*
Karla Zatzman Auerbach: *Someone like me*	*23*
Karla's Story	*24*
Sharon Edelson: *Bought and sold*	*33*
Sharon's Story	*34*
Linda Williams: *Found, but not acknowledged*	*39*
Linda's Story	*40*
Bernie Shiner and David Goodman: *So near and yet so far*	*45*
Bernie's and David's Story	*46*
Sharon O'Brien: *Nurse, heal thyself*	*51*
Sharon's Story	*52*
Kayla Greenspan: *Mind games*	*57*
Kayla's Story	*58*
Janice: *Please leave me alone*	*63*
Janice's Story	*64*

Kristin Blackburn: *One big, happy family*   69
    Kristin's Story   70

Ellen Jones: *A family gathered*   75
    Ellen's Story   76

Debra Dressler: *A spiritual awakening*   81
    Debra's Story   82

David Calder: *Olympic champion*   87
    David's Story   88

Mike Magee: *My mother's a star!*   101
    Mike's Story   102

Jeremy and Zahava   115
    Jeremy's Story   116
    Zahava's Story   119

AFTERWORD   121

ABOUT THE AUTHOR   125

ACKNOWLEDGEMENTS

So many people encouraged and helped me with this book, from its inception to the finished product! I thank all the people who told me about friends, acquaintances, family members, or interesting stories they had read about adoptees. I followed up on every lead and many of them resulted in the stories in this book.

I would like to thank Phyllis Thatcher, who insisted that I should write a book, telling me to "just write about what you know." I thank Wendy Swett, whom I met on only a couple of occasions at the golf course several years ago, but whose own story sparked the idea for this book; and whose friend Diane Groniger supplied one of the first stories—that of her husband, Tim.

I thank my dear friend Robin Pascoe, who encouraged me and mentored me on this project and has supported my writing for the past thirty years.

Twenty years ago, Louise Rachlis gave me a writing assignment to help kick-start my freelance career and since then has been an unwavering supporter of my career(s). She has also become a dear friend and an inspiration in other areas of my life.

I thank my children, Jeremy and Zahava, who had no hesitation in giving me the "go-ahead" with the book, for trusting me not to write anything that might be difficult for them to read about our own family. They both volunteered to contribute something and are proud of me for writing this book.

Of course, my mother, Marcia Koven, an author herself, is exceedingly proud of my effort, as she is of my every accomplishment, big or small.

Mothers and children, love and pride, emotions that bind families—no matter how the families are comprised—that's what the book is all about. I thank everyone who participated in bringing it to fruition and I thank everyone who reads it and enjoys it.

INTRODUCTION

A great many families have been touched by adoption, yet it is only in recent years that people have openly discussed it. Even now, it isn't something that one might readily include in a casual conversation or an introduction, as in, "Hi, my name is John and I'm adopted." Once I had decided to compile these stories, I began to tell people about my project and found that almost everyone I spoke to had a story to share or knew someone who did. The problem was not to find the stories, but to know when to stop collecting them.

It was difficult to decide when to say "enough." How many stories should I collect for this book? There was never any problem finding willing subjects; in fact, there seems to be no limit to the people willing to share their adoption stories.

My plan to just mention the book to anyone and everyone and wait for the stories to find me turned out to be very effective. Although I initially thought it would take me about a year to write the book, it has now been more than three years, and I could continue indefinitely. The stories in the book are not the only stories I have heard along the way, but, for various reasons, they are the ones I've chosen to include.

These people are, or have become, friends of mine. Most began as total strangers, yet all have willingly and freely shared with me the most private details of their lives. They have trusted me to hear things that sometimes surprised even them, feelings that had been long buried deep inside. I made it very clear to everyone at the outset that I am not a trained, professional counsellor and that I did not want to dredge up any unresolved issues or to upset anyone. No one resisted or held back. All initially agreed to let me use their names (though one woman later changed her mind—not for her sake, but to make sure certain family members would not be upset). In some stories, I decided to use only first names in order to respect the privacy of people other than the subjects.

I spent many hours interviewing each person. Every chapter in this book could be expanded to a book of its own; people shared their life's stories with me, but I had the difficult task of condensing each person's life to a single chapter.

Without exception, the people in this book are well-adjusted, successful, high-functioning members of society. Some have encountered more bumps in the road than others, but all were doing well when I met them. I had no preconceived notions of what I would discover along the way, but looking back, I have several observations to make.

Although as an adoptive mother it gives me great pain to say this, I believe from what I've heard over and over again that no matter how warm and loving the adoptive family is, it can't completely take the place of a birth family in a person's heart and mind. I think that every adoptee has, to some extent, a feeling of loss and, in many—if not most—cases, a feeling of rejection. Whatever the reason may be, the mother-child bond was severed when the mother "gave away" the child. Interestingly, almost nobody mentioned the birth father to me.

In some of these stories, the adoptee was able to locate his/her birth mother, but she would not agree to a meeting. These were the hardest stories for me to hear. To see the tears well up in the eyes of competent, responsible, successful adults because they felt—once again—a mother's rejection was heart-wrenching. It is my feeling, and I shared this with a couple of people, that the mother was not rejecting them because she didn't "want" them but because she herself had never recovered from the pain of giving away her child and still didn't feel capable of dealing with it. In many cases, the mother had gone on to marry and have other children and had never shared the fact that previously she had given birth to a baby and given it up for adoption. It would have been extremely disruptive and frightening to introduce this person to her family so late in life.

It was a great personal relief to discover that even in the stories that have happy, successful reunions with birth families, there seems to have been no damage to the adoptive family relationship. Everyone seems to feel that "family" is whom you live with and share your life with. The "new" family (birth family) members are like long-lost relatives who can be added to the family circle but don't replace anyone.

Most people, upon hearing the stories of their birth families and the circumstances under which they were given up for adoption, were grateful. They came to realize that they were given up with the hope that they would have a better life and more opportunities than the birth family was able to provide. In most cases, that turned out to be so.

Grandma and David.

David Sparks: Redemption

When my friend John celebrated his seventy-ninth birthday, I was invited to a small family barbecue at his home. It happened to be the very week that I had decided to embark on writing this book, so when he asked me what was new in my life, I was anxious to share my idea. I told him how I proposed to collect my stories by simply telling people about the book and waiting for the stories to find me.

To my surprise, John volunteered to help me—by including his own adoption story! "You were adopted?" I asked. I was surprised; things were very different eighty years ago; adoption was not so common and certainly not so openly known and discussed.

John grew up as the only child in a loving and privileged family. The word "adopted" was never mentioned and he had absolutely no idea that he was not his parents' biological son. When he was about to be married, his parents called him and his bride-to-be into the living room one day and told them the "news" that John had been adopted as an infant.

According to John, the most shocking thing about the discovery was not that he had been adopted, but that in all those years nobody had ever let the secret slip. He said he had grown up in a small, close-knit community where he assumed people would have been aware of his background and he could not imagine that in all those years the secret remained intact.

Of course, I asked John a million questions, thinking he would be a great candidate for inclusion in my book. It turned out otherwise. John had lived a very nice life with wonderful parents and was well adjusted and happy. He really had no curiosity or burning desire to search for his biological roots and, as he explained, he didn't think he would have been successful anyway, as the process nearly a century ago was much different than it is today.

When I said I didn't think there was much of a "story" there for my book, John suggested that perhaps I would rather speak to his daughter-in-law. Both she and her brother had also been adopted. Although Debbie had no interest in looking for her biological family, her brother David had done so and might be willing to speak to me.

The connection was made, and the next time David came to visit his sister, he called me and arranged to come over to my house and tell me his story. We had never met before, yet there was an instant connection and feeling of comfort. David started talking, and the time just flew by. I sat and listened with rapt attention as he told me about his childhood, his adolescence, and his search for the answer to a question that had always haunted him: "Who am I, really?"

David's Story

My sister and I were adopted—separately—by our parents when they were over forty. Dad had been married before. He had gone to war, and his wife died after he returned. Mom was a singer in a band and married late in life. She was very unusual for her time.

Mom was a very caring person, but Dad, though very accomplished, was cold and unemotional. I never really felt that I fit in in that family and always wondered about my biological family. I was rebellious as a child and as a teenager, unable and unwilling to please my father, who had high expectations of me.

As a child, I felt there was something wrong with me. Why would my mother give me up for adoption unless there was something wrong with me? And if not, then I must have come from something bad, and therefore I must be bad. It was worse when Dad said mean things, like, "Why did I get you for a son?" It is still a theme that haunts me from time to time and has caused me to have very low self-esteem.

By the time Dad passed away, Mom was suffering from Alzheimer's, so I felt it was okay for me to begin to search for my biological family. Before that, I didn't want to hurt Mom's feelings. I found my adoption papers in Dad's safety deposit box and learned, for the first time, what my name had been at birth. I asked my sister if she wanted her documents, but she said no. Unlike me, she has always been quite content with being who she is and has never felt any need to look further.

I filled out the forms and was told it would take about six months to get any information, but just two weeks later, I received a letter. My birth mother and a birth sister had both registered to meet me. Within three days of my submitting a letter requesting a meeting, it happened!

What I learned was that early in my birth parents' marriage, my mother became pregnant. Unfortunately, my birth father was "not mentally well" at that time, and my mother felt that her life had fallen apart. She asked her mother if she would take me when I was born, but her mother was quite ill and couldn't do it, so I guess it was somewhat of a last-minute decision to put me up for adoption.

Apparently, just a year later, my birth parents got back together and had four more children, so I found out that I have four siblings with the same blood line.

My birth father was killed in an industrial accident, so I never did get to meet him, but I met my birth mother and sister, and then the other siblings, one by one. I had been a family secret for many years and they had all hoped to find me. In fact, though my birth mother was a social worker (retired by the time we met) and could have had access to my records, she chose not to. In the end, two of my sisters hired a private investigator to find me, but were only able to get very limited information before I registered to meet them. They were warm and welcoming and so happy to have me "back" in the family.

At first, I enjoyed the attention and the affection from my

new-found family, but at the same time, it frightened me a bit. My adoptive father was not exactly a warm, fuzzy guy, and I wasn't used to all the hugging.

My sister Deb was always my dad's little princess. He treated her differently from how he treated me. He wanted me to be a football star, the CEO of a company. He set such high expectations for me that it scared me away from even trying. He was a big man, very physically active. He had been a lieutenant colonel in the Canadian army, and his father also had been in the military. Dad became president of a textile company and he really wanted me to be an extension of himself; but I didn't have aspirations to be who he wanted. I just wanted to be who I was. But who was I?

As a teen, I rebelled against my father's attempt to be controlling. At times, when I actually attempted to reach out to him, he quickly slammed the door. Looking back, I think he really did care about me but the only way he knew to show affection was by handing out money.

I was into drugs and alcohol, left school after Grade 12, and drifted for a few years. Eventually, I did go back to college, got married, and became a father. When the younger of our two boys was just a little over a year old, my wife took them and left me. Sadly, she was an alcoholic and had a succession of boyfriends, adding two more children along the way. Eventually, she set her apartment building on fire and ended up in jail. It wasn't a good environment for my sons, and I always hoped that they would come to live with me.

Sarah, my second wife, was a friend of ours and knew my boys. Since she and I got together, she has been a tremendous help to me in dealing with my adoption issues and with building a relationship with my birth family.

All of my birth family live in fairly close proximity to where I grew up in Ontario, so it has been quite easy for us to get together. Interestingly, my wife was going to a massage therapist who spoke to her about her ex-husband and her son. When a mutual friend of ours passed away, we met at the funeral. It turned out that the massage therapist's ex-husband was my biological brother!

Things are good for me now. My marriage is strong, and I've built a good relationship with my sons. I enjoy spending time with my birth family, and we get together for various occasions. But there are feelings that linger, that are harder to deal with. I have never liked my birthday, which is supposed to be a fun, happy day. I also had a lot of very deep anger, which I've worked through with counselling.

I think there is a lot of repressed anger in my birth family, as well. As much as they appear to be very loving, I sense there is a darkness they choose not to talk about.

Finding my biological roots has satisfied some of my childhood questions. I know whom I look like now, and in some areas, I know whom I take after. My adoptive father had no ability with his hands, but my biological father and his family did work with their hands, and that came very naturally to me. I took apart my tricycle when I was only five. We had a big garage, and I had a workbench and tools.

In some ways, I think I fared better than my birth siblings did because there are things I have learned about that family that I probably would have rebelled quite strongly against. In my adoptive family, there was money, so I had the opportunity to do a lot of things. With only the two of us children, there was just plain more opportunity to experience things in life. I think God had something in mind, there.

I am a born-again Christian, and that has helped me to deal with my situation. In the Bible, it says that the firstborn son is to be given over to God; I was a firstborn son, so my adoption seems to have been my destiny.

Tim and birth mom.

Tim Groniger:
I love my moms

Although not the first person I interviewed, Tim Groniger was the inspiration for this book. It was his wife, Diane, who had told me about him on a fateful, rainy day at the golf course when she and her friends were discussing their family adoption stories.

Diane told us that her mother-in-law would be coming to visit them on the farm for Thanksgiving, would stay for about a month, and would be doing all of the baking for the holidays. Apparently that had become a new family tradition, since her "original" mother-in-law had died a few years before, and Tim's birth mother had been found and welcomed into their family.

What a heartwarming story—I could almost smell the pumpkin pie and I could picture a sweet little grandmother in a pretty apron happily baking in a big, cheerful, farm kitchen.

I was hoping to visit the farm when Tim's mother was there, but scheduling didn't permit it. One thing and another seemed to hinder our meeting, and then, before we knew it, it was spring. Diane told me that Tim couldn't meet with me until the next fall because farming is a very time-intensive business: In the spring and summer, Tim was too busy to take time off for interviews.

Finally, the following autumn, I was able to arrange a meeting and drove out to Tim and Diane's dairy farm. I pulled up near the barn and was greeted by two barking dogs. I'm terrified of dogs and was afraid to get out of my car. Tim spotted me and came to my rescue, but I was very embarrassed to be meeting him under those circumstances. He was a good sport, though, and welcomed me warmly into his home and into his life.

Tim's Story

Tim is a middle-aged dairy farmer who loves what he does. He grew up on a farm in a rural community in Ontario, and for as long as he could remember, he dreamed of having a farm of his own.

"Cows are my life," says Tim. "When I first bought this farm, my father . . . was angry because I didn't take over his beef/cash crops farm. I love being a dairy farmer, but he couldn't accept it."

Tim's adoptive family is Dutch, and he grew up speaking Dutch. He has a brother who is six-feet-six-inches tall, and two sisters. Tim, who is considerably shorter and does not resemble his siblings in any way, is the only one who remained a farmer.

According to Tim, his adoptive parents had two children who died at birth. "They already had two girls and a boy and they had always wanted another boy. They got in touch with the Catholic Children's Aid in Cornwall, found a picture of me, and travelled to Hamilton to meet me." He said it took a year from that first enquiry until he arrived at their home. "It was a little farmhouse with an outhouse, pumped water, and cows. I was terrified of the animals; I had never seen a cow before!" He says he was there "on trial" for a year before his adoption was finalized.

Although Tim's childhood from then on was happy, and he loved, and felt loved by, his family, he always knew he was "different" and wondered about his birth family.

"I was the only one in school who was adopted and I was teased about it," he says; but at home things were very good and he was always comfortable. He was particularly close to his mother.

"My adoptive mom was always very open with me about adoption. She asked if I would like to look for my birth mother. I always wanted to, but it was only when I was forty that I started the search . . . I had four kids (two sets of twins) and I wondered who they look like and I was also concerned for their health, since I didn't know my history."

Searching for his birth mother was, says Tim, "a challenge for the whole family, but [my wife] Diane was very supportive." With the blessing of his adoptive mother, yet with trepidation, Tim began his search by contacting the adoption agency. Less than two months after receiving an official letter acknowledging his search, Tim received another letter from the ministry. He discovered that he had lived in foster homes until the age of five, apparently not happy experiences. He had completely blanked that period of time out of his memory, remembering instead a happy childhood on the farm. Apparently, he had arrived at the farm from the city "from a house with running water and a bathtub to a farm with a pump and a wood stove." The envelope he was sent also contained a letter from his birth mother.

Tim was nervous and emotional as he sat down to read the letter; over and over again, he read it. There was some basic information in it, but the name and address had been meticulously scratched out. It felt to Tim as though she still could not quite bring herself to meet him or reveal too much of herself.

Nevertheless, he replied with information about his life and family and included photos.

Almost two years passed before Tim's birth mother wrote again, this time disclosing her identity and address, and revealing to him that she had been forced to give him up at birth, although she loved him very much. Tim picked up the phone and called. When she answered, Tim said "I'm your lost son." It was a very emotional conversation for them both, but a good one. Contact had been made, and they were both ready for more.

In her third letter, Tim's birth mother told him that she and her husband would be coming to Ontario for a wedding and would like to come and meet him. They arrived at the farm bright and early on a summer morning. As the car pulled up in front of the barn and they got out, Tim heard them exclaim that he looked just like his mother, but with a goatee!

The reunion was a happy one, with everyone getting along well and clearly wanting to forge a relationship. Stories were told, tears were shed, and there were hugs all around.

Although Tim's adoptive father was not in favour of the reunion, the two mothers met twice and found much common ground—mainly in their shared love for "their" son, Tim.

"My birth mother is very much like my adoptive mother—very giving and loving," says Tim. They had many things in common: one was a nurse, the other a midwife; both enjoyed flowers and sewing.

"My birth mother made a quilt when each of her children was born. For some reason she had put away the very first one and kept it all these years—and presented it to me when we finally met."

Although his adoptive mother has died, her loss is made a bit easier by having his birth mother in his life. "I feel that I still have my mother, even though she is gone, through my birth mother," he says. "I think I am still living a fantasy through my birth mother . . . I know my mom is gone, but I feel her presence every day. We were always very, very close."

Tim's birth mother and her husband have become an important part of his family. For years, the annual tradition has been for them to come to the farm for Thanksgiving and stay for a month. She does all the Christmas baking while she's visiting. When they celebrated their forty-fifth wedding anniversary, Tim travelled to the celebration, meeting many of his birth family for the first time.

"It was emotional when it was time to make speeches," he says. "It was a whole new family, but I have been blessed to be welcomed into the family and we have become very close."

Tim says the two "sides" of his family have now all met and get along well. They've been able to share many family events such as birthdays and weddings. The only time he has felt uncomfortable and not quite part of things is at the anniversary parties for his birth mother and her husband. Everyone makes speeches, reminiscing about times he does not remember and events he did not attend—a gap in time when nobody even knew he existed.

But new family memories and connections are being made. One of his biological sisters lives in Australia, and one of Tim and Diane's daughters, Jessie, has been working and playing hockey there. It's difficult to be at the other end of the world, but Jessie and her aunt have forged a relationship and really bonded, which is a great comfort for her parents.

All in all, it has been a happy life, and finding his biological family has only enhanced it. Tim's search was not begun out of desperation or unhappiness, or even from a sense of not belonging. He had a loving family and a fulfilling life before and considers himself doubly blessed to have even more of the same now.

Thanh with his two dads.

Thanh Campbell:
An orphan no longer

When is an orphan not an orphan?

Try to imagine growing up as the only one who *looked* different in a large, "white" family. The one thing that is common to the interracial adoption experience seems to be that there is never any question about being adopted—as there sometimes is in families where everyone looks more or less the same.

There are several examples of such interracial adoptions in this anthology, and all of the adoptees share some of the same feelings; yet, being human beings, they all have their own individual takes on the situation as well.

These adoptees not only knew from day one that they were adopted, but often faced questions and comments from others—even perfect strangers—about who they were and how they came to be part of their families.

Consider the feeling of someone who was rescued as a baby from war-torn Vietnam, fortunate enough to be adopted into a warm and loving Canadian family, who grew up with a strong sense of being loved and accepted as part of this, his new family. Let your imagination wander just a bit further to this adoptee's adulthood, to marriage, and raising a biological family of his own, this family also by chance interracial. All is well, life is good, he is comfortable in his identity.

Then, a bolt from the blue: everything he had ever "known" about himself is turned upside down when he discovers, completely by chance, that he was never an orphan at all. The rescue and subsequent adoption were all a huge mistake; his biological family has been searching for him, hoping he is still alive, for thirty-five years.

When I initially read the story of Thanh Campbell, formerly Nguyen Ngoc Minh Thanh, also known as "Orphan 32" in my local newspaper, tears ran down my cheeks. The tears were for parents who had not only endured the horrors of the war in Vietnam but had lost their baby, never knowing if he was dead or alive; and, as an adoptive parent, I also felt deeply for his Canadian parents who had so warmly embraced that baby and brought him up with love and devotion, but now knew that they had unwittingly deprived him of life with his biological family. And, of course, I cried for Thanh himself, whose entire life had been built on the foundation of this terrible error; and who was probably asking himself one more time, "Who am I, really?"

Thanh's Story

In 1975, with the fall of Saigon imminent, people in Canada were opening their homes and hearts to the fortunate Vietnamese able to escape from the war-torn country. Individuals, families, and groups were finding ways to help these people find new homes and lives in our peaceful, comfortable country.

Among those kind Canadians were Rev. William Campbell, a Presbyterian minister, and his wife, Maureen, of Cambridge, Ontario. Although they already had five biological children, they welcomed a baby boy into their family, keeping his first name as recorded on the birth certificate tied to his wrist when he arrived. That baby, Thanh Campbell, had arrived at his new home by a series of events, both lucky and unlucky.

Nguyen Ngoc Minh Thanh, as his birth certificate identified him, was known as "Orphan 32," one of fifty-seven children rescued from an orphanage in Saigon, where he had been left with his two older brothers during the worst hostilities. Their parents feared for the children's safety and left them temporarily at the orphanage, where they hoped the boys would be well cared for until the war ended. Unfortunately, when they were finally able to return for the boys, only two were there. Thanh had been swept up in the rescue mission and taken to Canada in one of the last airlifts to North America.

For almost thirty years, Thanh assumed that he was an orphan but always wondered about his birth family and what circumstances had brought him to the orphanage. Did his parents die? Did they abandon him? Did he have any siblings? He was sure he would never know the answers to any of his questions because he felt certain that the birth certificate tied to his infant wrist was probably not even his.

He grew up, graduated from Redeemer University College, married, and became a father himself. He became a motivational speaker, travelling around Ontario and speaking to church groups about his life. One day, in 2003, an audience member approached him and said he knew someone whose story was very similar to Thanh's and who, he thought, must have arrived on the same flight from Saigon.

A telephone call proved that the two had, indeed, been on the same flight. They met, became friends, bonded by their shared experience. They decided to try to find the others who were on that flight, and by 2006, they had managed to locate forty-four of them. A reunion brought together thirty-five of their fellow plane-mates, as well as many of the people who had been involved in the rescue mission. The heartwarming story was well covered by media, including a Vietnamese magazine that included photos taken at the reunion.

Several months later, a most amazing thing happened. Thanh received an email from someone named Nguyen Ngoc Minh Thao, in broken English, telling him that he had seen his picture in the magazine and felt certain that Thanh was his long-lost brother. He said his father still has the original birth certificate and asked if Thanh might still have a copy of it.

Could this possibly be true? Was he *not* an orphan? Did he have a biological family alive and well and still looking for him? Yes to all of these questions! Eventually, DNA testing was done, proving that Thanh had indeed been found.

After corresponding and talking on the telephone—with the help of an interpreter, as Thanh did not speak Vietnamese—plans were underway for a reunion.

Finally, in May of 2009, the big day arrived. Thanh and his family (wife, Karina, and their four children), along with his father, Rev. Campbell, boarded a flight to Saigon. The "return" flight was a very different event from the one more than thirty years before. Thanh says,

> When I was thirteen, I asked Mom about the papers I had come with. She said they were probably not mine, so I lived for thirty-plus years assuming I was an orphan. When I found out that I actually do have parents, I didn't know how to reinvent my identity. I had identified myself as an orphan for so long. It was a hard thing to put a finger on. Who was I? I am a missing kid, but now I have a family, so I'm not missing anymore!
>
> I was estranged from my family, but through no fault of my own or their own. What I found as I met my family was that they had looked for me for thirty-two years! That just filled me with a whole new sense of value in who I was. My Campbell family always valued me, supported me, and loved me.
>
> When I first spoke to my father on the telephone, he wanted me to know that I was never abandoned, never given away, that it was a tragic mistake.
>
> It took a while for the feelings to slowly grow. It has been difficult to connect with a family with no common language, but there is an innate sense of belonging. With my four brothers, I felt like in some sense we were just away from each other. I am having a hard time communicating and difficulty learning the language, though.
>
> We "orphans" grew up in predominantly white families. We don't look like them but we speak, feel, and eat like them. In Vietnam, we look like them but we are as foreign as a white person. We don't really fit in anyplace. So when the forty-two of us got together, we finally had a time in life when we were with people who we really belonged with. We didn't have to say anything because we all really "got it."

My wife, Karina, is white, German, but our children look like me. All four children went to Vietnam with me and are happy to have a new grandpa, new uncles, and other new family members.

My adoptive father has been very supportive of my family reunion. He felt it was his responsibility to go with us to Vietnam to represent the Campbell family. Although the language barrier was difficult, both fathers had lost their wives, so they shared that experience as well and they got along very well. To have my birth father thank my adoptive father in person was very moving, a tribute to my dad.

I was so content with who I was and where I was, and grateful for where I was, I had never felt the need to search for my roots. When the option did come, my adoptive father was so happy. They had always been interested in my story and my background, always encouraged me not to forget where I came from.

I am not a different person now. This doesn't add or take away from who I am. I was complete before. Even if I had never met my birth family, I would have lived a very full life. I was grateful for the life I had. This experience of meeting my birth family is like sprinkles on an ice-cream sundae.

Karla at 18 years; Shirley at 20 years.

Karla Zatzman Auerbach: *Someone like me*

When my friend Shelley returned from spending a month in Florida, she called to let me know she was home. "You'll never guess who we saw there," she said. She had reconnected with a childhood friend from Halifax who had been living in the United States for many years. They had spent time together, catching up on their lives and "gossip" from back home.

"I told her about your book," said Shelley, knowing that Karla had been adopted. "Are you finished or do you want her email address? Do you have room for another story?"

Although I was, indeed, finished with my manuscript at the time, I was curious to hear Karla's story and to find out where life had taken her because I, too, had known her as a child and a teenager. Her parents and my aunt and uncle had been best friends and visited back and forth often.

I sent an email describing my project and asking if she would like to talk to me about it. Over the next few days, Karla and I spoke and exchanged many emails. She was very happy to participate and felt the time was right for her to share her story.

Karla's Story

From the time I was about two years old, when my mother was pregnant with my brother, Michael, I have known I was adopted. I remember rubbing my mom's belly and asking her about the baby growing there. That might be the reason I found out so very young about being special—just like the new baby was going to be special.

My childhood was wonderful. I had everything a little girl could ever want materially, as well as a big, warm, and loving family. When I was very young, my dad owned a grocery store in Dartmouth. Because we lived in Halifax, across the water, he left early in the morning and returned late at night, which meant he was not able to spend much time with me. My mom told me that he was unhappy with that arrangement, so he rented us an apartment over an old movie theatre, and we later moved to a home as business improved.

My family remained in Dartmouth, and my father became increasingly involved in the community, serving as an alderman for many years and eventually as a two-term mayor. My parents were always busy, socially and politically, but I cannot recall a summer going by that we all, as a family, did not take a vacation together—often to see grandparents in New Brunswick, always stopping to visit relatives and friends along the way. We spent Sundays visiting relatives in Halifax and got together with cousins often. I have wonderful childhood memories of being part of a close-knit family.

I left Halifax after graduating from high school and headed off to college in Boston, where I met Barry, who was to become my first husband. He was a student, working toward his Masters in Civil Engineering, which took us, right after our wedding, to Concord, New Hampshire. While Barry attended school, I got a job working for the State of New Hampshire in the agency that dealt with adoptions.

Until that time, although aware of being adopted, I had never really had any interest in the details or in my biological history. As "chance" would have it, the head of my department had recommended a book called *The Story of Anna Fischer*, about a girl searching for her birth father. I came across the book in the library where I worked and, though I found it interesting, I still didn't feel compelled to begin a search of my own.

As so often happens, it was the need for my medical history that eventually spurred me to action. Barry and I had three children, and all of them have been plagued by health issues. Heidi and Mindy both have scoliosis, and Andrew and Mindy suffer from severe asthma. I wanted to find out my medical history so that doctors would have some health background for my children. But where to begin?

I'm not sure why I saved *The Story of Anna Fischer*, but perhaps I had always known that curiosity would eventually get the best of me and I would search for my biological family. The book contained references for contacts in the United States, but since I was born in Canada, they were not of much use to me.

I did know that I was born at the Catherine Booth Hospital in Montreal, Quebec, but nothing more. My parents were reluctant to discuss my adoption and were extremely sensitive when I even tried to broach the subject. They said they knew nothing about my background. It upset my mom, so I never brought it up again. I knew I was going to be on my own if I were to continue the search.

I began by writing letters—to the Catherine Booth Hospital, Jewish Family Services (my parents had told me that my birth parents were Jewish), the Minister of Justice, Parent Finders. All resulted in dead ends, the first of many dead ends over what turned out to be a seven-year search.

While living temporarily back in Halifax, I happened to hear on the radio that the founder of the national Parent Finders organization was going to be lecturing that evening at the Capitol Theatre. Barry and I decided to attend. The speaker was riveting, but only a half hour into the talk, my beeper went off. Mindy was having a severe asthma attack, and we had to rush home and get her to the hospital. We missed the rest of the lecture, but a few days later, I wrote to the speaker, giving her a synopsis of my angst at being unable to find anything out but telling her she had inspired me to join the local Parent Finders chapter, which we did.

The meetings were so interesting, the stories so similar. It seemed that everyone wanted to know why they were given up, whom they look like, whether they have any biological siblings. Some of the stories were good, some not so good, but it was encouraging to hear of successful reunions.

In the meantime, my own search was still going nowhere. I had contacted two lawyers by now, both of whom were relatives and felt they had a conflict of interest. I contacted Parent Finders in Montreal, hoping they could help; but nothing bore fruit.

With Mindy's health deteriorating, Barry and I made the decision to move our family to Arizona in the hope that the dry climate would help our two asthmatic children. For the time being, my adoption search was put on hold as we settled into our new routine.

Then, out of the blue, and from a most unexpected source, came my first solid lead. After five years of fruitless questions, I finally had an answer. My letter to the woman from Parent Finders, the speaker whose talk we had mostly missed, had apparently inspired her to do some detective work on my behalf. She found our new phone number through the local Parent Finders chapter and called to tell me about her results. "Are you sitting down?" she asked. "I have the name and phone number of a maternal grandfather." Stunned, I grabbed a pen and a piece of paper. Thus began another chapter in my search.

My initial elation gave way to more frustration as I tried in vain to find my "grandfather." Of course, I began by writing to the address I had been given, but received no response. There were no computers at the time, so every step in the process was slow and tedious. I visited the library, got names and addresses of everyone with the same family name, wrote to all of them. I made up stories in the hope of eliciting a response—pretending I had seen someone on a television program about the Holocaust who might be my grandfather. "Is it you?" I asked in each letter. I tried, through a third lawyer in Montreal, to have my birth records opened; but to no avail.

In the meantime, Heidi's health was deteriorating. At the age of seven, she required a back brace and would, perhaps, require surgery. The doctor felt that knowing her medical history would help determine a possible timeline for the dreaded surgery. I had been diagnosed with scoliosis myself at the age of twelve, but what about MY family history?

Feeling desperate, I once again contacted the lawyer in Montreal and prevailed upon her to try one more time to have the judge allow my records to be opened so that we could have the all-important medical history. Amazingly, this time she was successful. I not only had my grandfather's name, but now I also had the name of my birth mother!

My seven-year search was nearing its end. Thoughts swirled in my head: Would I meet her? What would she tell me? Questions I never thought I would care about came quickly to mind: Why had she given me up? Who was my birth father? Do I have birth siblings? Cousins? Curiosity I had never acknowledged, even to myself, was taking over, and I felt the need to know everything.

What I did NOT feel, even for a moment, was that I had found my "mother." My parents were the people who had raised me, who loved me, and whom I loved; my brother was my brother, my aunts, uncles, cousins were my family.

Starting once again with my list of five names from the Montreal telephone directory, I embarked on the final leg of the search. Barry, who had been so supportive throughout the process, was my partner in its conclusion. Remembering what we had learned from Parent Finders—that initial contact should be made by someone other than me, in order not to frighten the person on the telephone—we decided that Barry should be the one to make the calls. Of course, I was sitting by his side, listening intently as he began by calling a Montreal operator and enlisting her help.

One by one, the calls were placed and the answers were all the same. Three answers, all negative; two calls unanswered. Before calling it a night, we decided to again try the two numbers that had not been answered. The phone rang, and an elderly man answered. Yes, he was the person bearing my maternal grandfather's name, but he did not recognize the name of the woman we had identified as my birth mother. "No," he said, "I don't know anyone by that name. Oh, wait a minute. Do you mean Shirley? Hold on, let me get her number."

Shirley? Who was Shirley? That was not the name we had been given for my birth mother, but since the man's name matched that of my grandfather, we decided to call this Shirley and see if she could help us. We tried calling, but there was no answer. Two hours later, unwilling to wait even one more day to find her, we dialed one more time. This time, a woman answered. As he had been coached by Parent Finders, Barry introduced himself. "Hi, my name is Barry and I married a girl born on January 18, 1948, in the Catherine Booth Hospital in Montreal, Quebec. We are searching for her birth mother and wonder if you can help us." There was a long pause. My heart was palpitating, my throat was dry. I sat beside Barry wondering what the person on the other end would answer. Quietly, the voice said, "How did you find me?" Barry started to cry. I began to shake as he nodded his head up and down to indicate that we had found my birth mother; then he asked her to please not hang up.

They spoke for an hour and a half. I could not hear her side, but she kept asking questions about me, through Barry. She said she was nervous and did not want to speak with me just then. He shared the fact that we had been looking for seven years, about our kids, about wanting medical history. She said there was no family history of scoliosis or asthma. At one point, she asked him to describe what I looked like. When he was done, she simply replied, "Yes, that's mine." Finally, she said she was ready to speak with me. The moment I had waited for had arrived.

I remember feeling like I was in a dream. This person I was speaking with was the person who carried me in her womb for nine months. Why was I not feeling a connection other than it was a lady telling me things about herself? I wanted all the information about everything in this conversation. For all I knew, I would never speak with her again, because maybe she did not want her family to know about me. But we continued to talk—about her family, my family, her (deceased) husband, who was not my birth father. He was in the same profession as my husband. She said he would have been so pleased to know I had found her. They had decided not to have children because she carried the guilt of having given up a child for adoption.

My birth father had been a good friend of the family's, she said, but when she became pregnant, she did not see him again. Her father was angry and had kicked her out of the house; she had moved in with an older brother until after I was born. An older sister, living in New York, took her in after my birth in Montreal and the adoption papers were signed. She did not want to see me at birth, afraid she would change her mind, but knew I was a girl. She was sad, but in those days, being single, pregnant, and Jewish, she felt she had no options.

I was surprised to find out that both of my birth parents were Jewish. I had often asked my mom if I was Jewish when they "got me." She said it had been a private adoption to ensure just that, but she never elaborated or shared any other information. Until my birth mother confirmed this, I had not realized just how important it had really been to me.

Shirley told me that she had remained in New York City, close to her sister, met and married a man, became a career woman, and went on with her life. Her name was totally different from the one noted in the birth certificate but she had been called Shirley her whole life. No wonder her father did not recognize the name we asked for. It turns out he was eighty-two at the time of our call to him.

Shirley and I began to exchange letters and photos, trying to catch up with thirty-one years of separation, to learn everything about each other. When I looked at her picture, I could not believe how much I looked like her—the colouring, the build, the expression. I really did look like someone! I was amazed at how much we resembled one another, and how much alike we seemed to be in other ways as well. We shared an interest in reading, even down to the types of books we enjoyed; her hobbies, likes and dislikes. It was fascinating!

Within a month, Shirley and one of her sisters (hers was a family of six siblings) flew to Arizona to meet and visit with us. Meeting day, many letters and phone calls later, was one to remember.

The plane landed and I was very nervous. We knew what she looked like, so Barry and I kept a watchful eye on all the passengers disembarking from the plane. Those were still the days when people stepped down right onto the tarmac. No one I could recognize was getting off. I did not recognize her when she came out that exit, but saw a person behind who looked familiar. It turns out, her sister had a similar hairstyle to mine and she was the one who caught my eye first. I was getting more and more nervous. What was I going to say? They came through the door. I knew, immediately, who she was. I walked over, hugged her, welcomed her to Tucson, put my arm around her shoulder as we began walking, and first thing out of my mouth was: "So, what have you been doing the past thirty-one years?" That broke the ice. We had reconnected.

Over the next twenty-five years, Shirley and I developed a very nice relationship. We continued to correspond and were able to visit many times. Getting to know her was very special—our personalities were quite similar, and I often wondered, had we lived under one roof, how we would have gotten along. I liked her very much and was happy that she allowed my children and me to become a part of her life, as she became a part of ours. I never felt that we had a mother-child bond, but enjoyed knowing her as a person and a friend.

They are all gone now, both of my parents and Shirley, my birth mother. They never did meet. My parents remained uncomfortable with even discussing my adoption, and I did not want to hurt them or do anything that might make them think I didn't love or appreciate them for all they had done for me. I love knowing that I look like someone and have remained in touch with some of my biological relatives; but my parents were my parents, my brother is my brother, and that will never change.

Sharon with her two children.

Sharon Edelson:
Bought and Sold

I was relaxing and enjoying a nice cup of tea, reading a magazine, and generally not thinking of anything "productive," when the telephone rang one evening. I didn't feel like answering it but, as I don't have Caller ID, I couldn't automatically assume it was nothing important; so, on the last ring, I lunged for the receiver.

"Have I got a story for you!" said Barb, breathlessly. "You won't believe this!"

Barb and I are not close personal friends; she is a business acquaintance, and we had never called each other at home or spoken about personal matters. I had, however, let her know about this book and that I was seeking stories for inclusion. It was in that context that she was calling and she could hardly get the words out fast enough.

It seems that she had been getting out of the car in her driveway and stopped to chat for a few minutes with her next-door neighbour, whom she had known for several years. Until then, however, she hadn't known that the woman was adopted; and it isn't clear how the topic arose on that fateful day. What is clear is that this was no "ordinary" adoption story.

Barb told her neighbour about me and my book and asked permission to have me call her. Sharon was eager to speak with me and told Barb to give me her telephone number. When I heard the story (just the "headlines," so to speak), I could hardly wait to meet this woman. Fortunately, she lived very close to me and was happy to have me drop by any time.

When I arrived at Sharon's home, she led me to her

kitchen, where the table was laden with piles of newspaper clippings, photos, letters, and notes related to her adoption search. Unfortunately, the more she learned, the more certain she had become that she would—and could—never find out who her biological family was. Her search did, however, bring her into contact with a number of people who were "in the same boat" and whose stories intertwined with her own.

First, let's meet Sharon and find out a bit about her; then we'll explore the deep, dark secret of her adoption.

Sharon's Story

Those of us who grew up in our biological families may wonder how it would feel to know we were adopted, but can anyone even imagine how it would feel to discover you were *sold* to your adoptive parents?

That's what Sharon and hundreds of others found out when they launched their searches for their biological families. Sharon knew that she had been born in Montreal and that her parents adopted her and took her "home" to another city the very next day. Growing up, that hadn't struck her as all that unusual; but she realizes now that taking a one-day-old baby on a train trip was not a regular occurrence.

It was the stuff of cops and robbers, quite literally. Sharon discovered that she most certainly had been adopted through an international adoption ring dealing in black market babies. The ring was active, using Montreal as its base of operations, for a decade spanning the 1940s and 1950s. It was huge, involving a network of doctors, lawyers, and social service workers. And millions of dollars changed hands.

According to a newspaper account dated February 13, 1954, detailing how a sting operation had yielded a number of arrests, this is how it worked:

> A family wishing to adopt a child in New York would contact a lawyer there who would subsequently refer

them to the Montreal source. The couple would come to Montreal and the financial details of the transaction would be agreed upon.

Then the ring would obtain a baby from an establishment for unwed mothers. In some cases, the real mothers were given small amounts of money, but in others, the babies were merely taken without their consent.

Once obtained, the baby would be delivered to its destination in the United States, usually in one of two ways.

One was for a girl courier to literally smuggle the child across the border by "bluffing" her way past immigration authorities.

The second method was by providing the baby with a visa and passport that had been obtained here by falsification of names.[1]

Because there were no paper records, no proper documentation and many people involved, there was no way to trace the children back to the biological mothers. As time went on and participants died or "disappeared," it became completely impossible; therefore, by the time any of these adopted children were old enough to begin an adoption search, the search was completely futile.

In Sharon's case, this is just an interesting "story," and has not had a negative impact on her life or sense of identity. She is remarkably matter-of-fact as she relates the details to me on a sunny autumn day in the kitchen of her cozy, beautifully decorated suburban home.

"Most of these couples were in their late thirties or forties and had been unable to have children of their own," she said. "My father was forty when my parents married, and my mother was thirty-six . . . I remember a book called *Chosen Child* and I always felt special. It never bothered me [being adopted]."

Sharon and her younger sister (also adopted) lived a very

---
1   *Montreal Gazette*, Feb. 13, 1954.

pleasant life with warm and loving parents. "I had ballet and piano lessons. We had cousins in New York and went there often. We had an uncle who had a farm and we used to go there to swim. I had a very happy childhood."

Life progressed and Sharon eventually formed her own nuclear, biological family. "After high school, I worked in administration at a local hospital for a couple of years, then got married and started having children—a boy and a girl.

"I always had a curiosity [about being adopted] but never really asked my mother much because I didn't want to hurt her feelings. When my mother died, the first thing I looked for were papers about my adoption. It was the only thing I wanted ... that's how I found out about the black market.

"I don't think they were doing anything wrong," said Sharon. "They tried to help the unwed mothers who could not keep their children. It was illegal in Quebec to adopt across religious lines."

Ironically, that law seems to be the basis for the "success" of the adoption ring. In those days, it was a big disgrace for unmarried French-Canadian Catholic girls to become pregnant. Many hid their pregnancies or were sent away "to care for an elderly aunt" until after the babies were born. They couldn't keep the babies, but often had nowhere to turn for help or support.

On the other hand, because of the law that prohibited Jewish couples from adopting Catholic children in Quebec, it was also impossible for these willing, suitable couples to legally adopt these babies. It was a "perfect storm"; a black market waiting to happen.

As word spread that babies were available in Montreal, couples from nearby New York—and then, increasingly, from other parts of the United States—were anxious to adopt them. Most of the couples were Jewish, as they were often unable to adopt through traditional channels.

Sharon began her personal search in 1998 after her mother died. "I knew then that I came from the Rabinovitch Clinic, because the telephone number was in my mother's telephone book," she said. She spent a lot of time combing the Internet site of a group called "Canadopt" for names that "sounded Jewish," or whose stories sounded similar to hers; and by Mother's Day of 1998, a group of ten people with similar "stories" got together and met with a lawyer who they hoped would help them in their search. "When we told him the story, he was flabbergasted and called an older member of his law firm who confirmed that the story [of the black market adoption ring] was true." Unfortunately, nothing came of that meeting, as the trail was definitely cold.

Questions of who she "really is" do not haunt Sharon. She is well-adjusted, self-confident, and secure. Even though she knows that she was almost certainly born to a French-Canadian Catholic mother and she was brought up in a Jewish family, she does not feel "torn." "My family always belonged to the local Conservative synagogue and we were never asked any questions [about my origins]. I was married in the synagogue and it was always accepted that I was Jewish."

Her hobby—really her passion—is genealogy; she has compiled family trees for both sides of her (adoptive) family and is constantly on the hunt for more information.

Linda with her two sons, Dennis and Darrin, at her 57th birthday party.

Linda Williams:
Found, but not acknowledged

Every Wednesday morning for the past several years, I have been having breakfast with Michele and a few other business and professional colleagues in my neighbourhood. Michele's real estate office is right next door to the restaurant where we meet. One morning, she took me aside and said I *must* meet Linda, a fellow real estate agent in her office. "Linda has an absolutely amazing story," she said, "and it's just what you're looking for for your adoption book."

Of course, I was anxious to hear the story and arranged to meet Linda as soon as possible. I spoke with her on the telephone and invited her to my home, where we would be able to speak freely and privately. She's a very attractive, vivacious, and friendly woman who happily and willingly shared her story with me. When she had finished talking, I was in awe of her attitude and positive outlook. In her place, I think I would have been frustrated, angry, bitter, and very, very sad; but it is a testament to her character that she is able to be philosophical and accepting of how things have turned out.

Linda's Story

Linda enjoyed a happy childhood in a big, loving, extended family with lots of cousins and friendly neighbours. Her parents, who married late in life and were unable to have children, were foster parents before adopting Linda, and, five years later, her younger sister.

Both of Linda's parents were from large families—her father was one of thirteen children, and her mother came from a family of eleven, so there were always lots of kids around the house. "It was such a fun place to be," she says. "Everyone always came to our house."

What the family lacked in material comforts was more than balanced by the warmth and affection that enveloped Linda and her sister. "My mother stayed home, and Dad was a handyman/carpenter. We had very modest means, but everything we ever needed. Growing up in the country, I remember when we put in indoor plumbing and I remember having a bath on Saturday night," says Linda—a far cry from where she finds herself in middle age as a successful real estate broker, homeowner, and parent to two young adults.

Life in small-town Ontario was, in most ways, a supportive and nurturing environment to grow up in, but in her school, where everyone knew everyone and all the other kids were fair-skinned with straight brown hair, Linda stood out. She always felt that she was "different," and her schoolmates often teased her about her dark, curly hair and olive complexion. By the time she had reached her mid-thirties, with two failed marriages behind her, Linda decided to register with the Children's Aid Society (CAS) to try to find her birth parents and to see for herself why she looked the way she did.

"I never told my parents I was looking for my birth family because I didn't want to hurt them. I had children already and wanted some medical information and also to know who I look like," says Linda.

A ten-year wait yielded results—both good and bad. The good news was that the CAS located both of Linda's birth parents. The bad news was that they both refused to have any contact with her. "When both of my birth parents refused any contact, the only thing left for me was to write to the CAS and ask for any and all non-identifying information."

"The adoption registry said she [my birth mother] was married to an Armenian and had two sons and one daughter . . . I had never known my birth weight, but found it was nine pounds . . . that made me cry!"

Sometime later, while working on registration and administration for a life insurance course, Linda met a man who had the same family name as her birth family and who came from the same area as they did. "I introduced myself to him and asked him some questions to find out if he might be a relative." The man was friendly, kind, and forthcoming with information; he was, indeed, a relative. "I found out three sisters' names from him and just figured things out by the names," said Linda.

In November 2008, another "coincidence" provided Linda with more information. "When I was taking my real estate brokerage course, we had a substitute instructor who also had the same family name. Though living in Toronto, he was originally from the same small town that my birth family lived in. The first day, I walked up to him and asked him if he knew the three sisters whose names I had, and he said yes!"

So many years of wondering, waiting, and frustration seemed about to end. Linda had made contact with someone who really knew her birth family, a distant cousin himself, someone who was willing to help her connect with them.

"I Googled her name that day and could have gone to meet her," said Linda of her birth mother, but she decided to wait until the time was right. She had waited so long, she wanted to be sure that the reunion would work.

Unfortunately, fate had other ideas. "Within two weeks of that discussion," said Linda, "she and her husband were killed in a car accident."

"My reaction was so strong when I heard about the accident. It was almost not real because it happened so quickly. Why didn't I go down? I could have even just sat outside her house and looked at her; I didn't even have to speak to her—but it was too late!"

When Linda told me this story, while sitting at my kitchen table, she was very calm and philosophical. In spite of the fact that she had waited a lifetime to find her birth parents and had been so close to actually meeting them, she accepted that the meeting was not meant to be.

Still hoping to at least meet the rest of her birth family, she pursued her leads but has, so far, not had any success. She was a deep, dark secret and none of the birth relatives have shown any interest or willingness to meet her or accept that she is who she says she is. This has, perhaps, been the hardest part of her journey—the rejection and denial of her very existence. She hasn't given up, but she is dealing with it as well as she can and living the life she has.

David Goodman and Bernie Shiner.

Bernie Shiner and David Goodman: So near and yet so far

As a freelance correspondent for *The Canadian Jewish News*, I am also a subscriber to its national edition and usually read the paper from cover to cover. On one particular day, however, as I took the newspaper from my mailbox, the headline of a front-page story caught my eye: "Jewish adoptee finds biological brother," and stopped me in my tracks.

I immediately sat down to read the story and, upon finishing it, could hardly wait to speak to Bernie Shiner, the story's subject. There was no mystery and no difficulty in finding him, as he had already told his story publicly and appeared in the newspaper, photo and all.

Bernie and I are the same age and, coincidentally, in the same business—insurance. Even without the adoption story, we would have had lots to talk about, so our "connection" was instant when I introduced myself to him on the telephone. We had a long and very interesting conversation as he told me his story—both what I had already read and much more that had not appeared in print.

At one point, Bernie paused. I thought the telephone connection had been broken until he started to speak again, in a choking voice, and said, "I'm sorry, but fifty-four years later, I still get very emotional when I talk about this." At that point, he had been telling me how much his adoptive parents had loved him and how devoted he had always been to them because of it; as an adoptive parent, I then broke into tears myself. We had a good cry and laugh together and then Bernie continued with his story.

Bernie's and David's Story

"My life is a work in progress," said David when I asked him to tell me about himself. He and his brother, Bernie, and I were meeting for the first time. I had, by then, spoken to Bernie a couple of times on the telephone and I knew their basic story from the newspaper article that had brought them to my attention, but this was my first interaction with David. I wanted to get to know him a bit and to hear the story from his point of view.

By the time I met them, Bernie and David had known each other for a couple of years and had developed a comfortable relationship. They were still getting to know each other and still getting used to even knowing "about" each other, each having grown from childhood to middle age thinking he was an only child. Although it was David who said he had always wished for a sibling and dreamed of having a brother, at our meeting, I noticed that Bernie seemed to revel in the sibling relationship, referring often to "my brother" this and "my brother" that, as if even saying those words made him feel good.

As Bernie had told me already, the basic facts of his adoption story were thus: He had been adopted at the age of four by a nice Jewish couple in Toronto. His first few years had been difficult. Shortly after arriving in his new home, he had an accident and ended up spending most of the first year in hospital, where, in thirteen months, he underwent thirteen surgeries!

"The problem they had back in the 'fifties was that they used heavy gauze bandages to close incisions made during surgery. When they went to take them off, inevitably the skin would separate from the stiches and another operation would be in order. As I had three different incisions, you can understand how I would have thirteen operations. My issues were a ruptured spleen, split colon, triple hernia and broken legs and arm. Other than that, I was in perfect health!

"I was in the Mount Sinai Hospital for approximately three months and then next door at Sick Kids hospital for a little over ten months. The last month I spent at home with a tent over my body, as part of my intestine was outside my body. I then went back to the hospital, where the doctor shoved it back in and sewed me up. I do recollect this day quite vividly."

Those were the days before socialized medicine, and, he says, his new parents were saddled with huge medical expenses—even before the paperwork for the adoption had been completed. "I don't know how much each operation cost, but there was also a charge for blood. The community came in and donated blood in my name, so I was given credit for the number of units that were donated. I was told that there was a period of a month's length where it looked like I was a goner, so my parents hired on a twenty-four-hour nurse to be with me—again, paid for by them. As adoption papers were not finalized for one year, my parents could have said goodbye and not have any responsibility for me. They did not, and they hung in with me."

Bernie's parents never wavered in their commitment to their new son; willingly and lovingly paid the bills and stayed by his side until he recovered; and had their friends and faith community pray for him.

"I will never, ever forget what my parents did for me," said Bernie. "Because of the unconditional love they showed me from the very beginning, I never had the slightest desire to seek out my biological parents."

Bernie was well into middle age when, prompted by a medical concern, he decided to contact the adoption authorities to see if he could locate his birth mother. A lengthy search proved unsuccessful but yielded a great surprise. He received a letter advising him that there was no medical history available but informing him that he had a brother. "A brother? I have a brother?" The thought had never entered Bernie's mind that he might have a sibling.

David, five years younger than Bernie, had been adopted by another Jewish couple and grown up as an adored and pampered only child not far from Bernie's family in Toronto. He, too, had a happy childhood and loved his parents very much. Though he had no desire to search for his biological parents, he had been curious and he especially wondered if he had any siblings. Being an only child, he often thought it would be nice to have a brother; so, in 1990, he registered with the adoption registry. At that time, the only way for contact to be made would have been if any of his biological family had also registered. Nobody had.

It took nearly twenty years until that fateful day when Bernie received the letter informing him he had a brother. The telephone number listed on the official documents was long out of service. Calls to 411 and an Internet search yielded no results, but Bernie opened a Toronto telephone book and looked for his brother's number. He tried the first number listed with his brother's last name and struck gold—it was his brother David.

Bernie's call was a bolt out of the blue for David, who needed some time to digest the news. A few weeks later, they met at a coffee shop and were immediately struck by how little physical resemblance there was. They do have some similar personality traits, however—notably a sense of humour and "gift of the gab." They talked for hours and knew they would meet again.

When I first heard this story from Bernie, this was as far as it had gone. Now, over a year later, when the three of us sat down to talk, I asked him if there had been any new developments. "How long do you have?" he asked. There were, indeed, further developments.

"The government had a program that allowed you to find your birth mother as long as she did not block it. When I received the information, I looked up her last name in the phone book and there was only one. I called it and it happened to be my birth mother's stepsister. She gave me the phone numbers for my mother's brother and my older stepsister, and I called them."

A brother had, unfortunately, died at around the time that they had originally found each other, but they found two younger sisters. They contacted the older of the two sisters, who told them that their birth mother also had died, several years ago. The two sisters and two brothers met at a coffee shop (thank goodness for Tim Hortons, the home of coffee, doughnuts and family drama!) and spent three hours talking and getting to know one another.

"The two of us felt we had been hit by a freight train," said Bernie. Apparently, after giving David up for adoption, their birth mother married and had three more children. She never mentioned her past, and they had no idea that there were two siblings "out there," so the sisters also were shocked by the reunion. "After meeting them, we felt we had turned their lives upside down," said Bernie.

He invited them and their families—and David and his children and elderly father—over for a Sunday lunch so everyone could get to know each other. Aside from a slight physical resemblance between Bernie and the sisters, the two brothers said there was really no "connection," and they felt they had nothing in common with their new-found siblings.

Although they all shared the same birth mother, who had been Jewish, their lives had been dramatically different. The mother had married someone who was not Jewish, and her family did not follow the traditions. In fact, the sisters were not even aware that they are, according to Judaism, Jewish.

Interestingly, when their mother had given up her first two children for adoption, she had done so through the Jewish adoption agency so that they would be adopted by Jewish families. Both Bernie and David had been immersed in the culture, though Bernie and his family are far more religiously observant, and David considers himself more of a "cultural" Jew.

"Who am I, really?" Both Bernie and David feel that environment plays a crucial role in helping a person become who he or she is "meant to be" and both are extremely grateful for the upbringing they received. Neither feels any real connection to their biological family and both feel very strong love and respect for their adoptive parents.

"It is definitely your environment that makes you who you are," said Bernie. "I went to Hebrew day school. All of my friends were Jewish. Your parents are successful, you are pushed toward education. It is all part of the way you are brought up."

David readily agreed. For example, he said, "I can be kind of lazy. If I had remained with [my birth family], I would definitely not have had higher education. There is absolutely no way I would have been who I am. My mother pushed me to higher education . . . I used to go to the symphony when my mother was alive; I love the theatre."

"Thank G–d we were adopted," said Bernie. David wholeheartedly agreed.

Sharon with her brother.

Sharon O'Brien:
Nurse, heal thyself

Shortly after I began to tell people I was looking for stories for this book, my mother called to say she had bumped into an old high school friend of mine. This woman had been living abroad for many years, but returns to Saint John frequently to visit her family, and it was on one such visit that my mother stopped to chat with her. Remembering that she had been an adopted child, my mother told her about my book and asked if she might like to share her story with me. My friend gave her an email address, and I got in touch with her.

Unfortunately, this friend decided that she wasn't comfortable sharing her story but suggested a friend of hers who might. I contacted her friend, Sharon, and we began a fruitful email correspondence.

At around the same time, I had lunch with a woman I had recently met while serving as a board member for our local hospice. Janet is also from my hometown and we had many things in common.

During that lunch, Janet mentioned that she was going "home" for a visit to help move her elderly mother into a seniors' residence, as it had become too difficult for her to live on her own. Janet had done extensive research and found what turned out to be a most satisfactory facility. My own parents were still living in Saint John and were doing quite well, although my father was approaching ninety years old and becoming quite frail.

Several months later, it was apparent that although my mother was taking care of my father and insisted that she didn't need any help, she was exhausted. The caregiving role was very demanding, and she wasn't able to get any "time off," as neither I nor any of my siblings lived nearby.

I called Janet and asked if we could meet again to discuss possible caregiving alternatives in Saint John, and she was happy to oblige. She gave me a list of places to call but strongly suggested I contact a friend of hers who owns a seniors' support agency. That very evening, while reading my latest email from Sharon, I noticed the email signature at the end; it was the name of the agency owned by Janet's friend. I called Sharon and asked her about it—it turned out that she is the co-owner of the agency! I then asked her to please help me professionally and she was able to provide my family with good quality care for my father for the next year until he passed away.

I really believe that there are no coincidences in life and that things do happen for a reason.

Sharon's Story

There is no doubt that being adopted has had a profound effect on me. My sense of self, my relationships with others, my ability to love and be loved have all been shaped by that most basic feeling of belonging—or not. Fear of abandonment, of not being "good enough," of not being "the real thing" have coloured so many aspects of my life. It has taken me many years of soul-searching, the encouragement and support of good friends, professional success, and loving children to bring me to a place of peace in this, my seventieth decade of life.

My life, like many others, has been touched by tragedy and turmoil. I lost a young son in a drowning accident, lived through a difficult marriage that eventually ended in divorce, and supported my two remaining children as a struggling single mother. Most recently, I have fought perhaps my toughest battle, against a major illness, which has given me pause to look back at my life and wonder . . .

Because I was adopted, I tended to attribute so many of my family "issues" to the fact that my parents were not my "real" parents. As I think about it now, I wonder if that was just an easy way to explain things away. After all, every family has issues, and even within a biological family, there are relationships that work and those that just don't. There are parents whose expectations of their children are too high or unrealistic. There are children who rebel. Sometimes the parents themselves do not get along well, causing tension and friction in the household. In short, there are as many different family scenarios as there are families.

As a nurse, a nursing professor, and finally owner of a successful private company that provides health care professionals for seniors, I have certainly achieved success by any measure. I have also spent a lifetime nurturing people—both professionally and in my own nuclear family. Looking back at what I now know about my early life, I know that this is not a coincidence.

In 1985, I gave permission to have my adoption records opened should an inquiry be made about my possible existence. I know that sounds strange, but I really always wondered if anyone "out there" even remembered my birth, if anyone cared that I was born, if anyone was looking for me. Well, someone was looking for me: a woman who turned out to be my older half-sister. I had apparently been the second child born out of wedlock to our birth mother, from different fathers. A meeting was arranged, on "neutral ground" in a hotel in the presence of a social worker.

My sister was very excited to meet me. She smothered me with hugs, something I was not used to and found a bit frightening. My adoptive family had been undemonstrative, rather cold. She couldn't wait for me to meet her husband, her children, her friends. She arranged get-togethers, arrived at my home before Christmas with bags bulging with gifts; at that time, I was unable to reciprocate or even provide my own children with much, so the generosity made me very uncomfortable.

Basically, although she was a nice person, and we did in some ways resemble one another, this woman did not feel like family to me. I found it difficult to maintain a relationship with her because we really had no other common connection except for being born to the same woman so many years before. Our lives had been vastly different. She had been adopted as a newborn and enjoyed a happy, privileged upbringing. My early years were not so simple.

I learned that I had spent the first two years of life in an orphanage. Apparently, at some point during that time, my birth mother had returned to take me home but once again found she was unable to care for me and took me back to the orphanage. I'm sure that my feelings of fear of rejection stem from being left twice by the person who should have wanted me most.

With information I obtained in my search, I was able to locate a telephone number for my birth mother. One evening, I called her. With my heart beating wildly, after confirming her identity, I asked if she might be my mother. I gave her the date and place of my birth and waited . . . there was a long silence, and then she said, simply, "I don't remember the date, but yes." I wanted so much for her to say "I often think of you. I wondered what happened to you. I always think of you on your birthday and wonder what you look like," but she said nothing. When I told her that I had met her first child, my half-sister, she flatly denied ever having her.

My birth mother did not suggest a meeting, and I assured her I would not appear on her doorstep. She did tell me that she had married and had seven more children.. From being an only child, I was suddenly one of nine! She also told me that her eldest daughter (of the seven) had recently died of breast cancer (which I was later diagnosed with as well).

My half-sister was extremely upset when I told her that our mother denied having given birth to her and said she would never contact her or any member of her family. She did, however, inform me shortly afterward that she had heard that our birth mother had died. Something within me felt bruised, disconnected. Another part of me was very grateful that I had taken the opportunity to speak with my birth mother and to tell her that I forgave her. I knew she had done what she thought was best for me; she had told me she had tried to care for me but wasn't able to. I didn't ask why. I just felt it was important for her to know that I was okay.

My adoptive parents were supportive of my search for and meeting with my half-sister, but when I told my mother that I had spoken to my birth mother, she was furious. How could I hurt her like that? Did I hate her so much? Though I assured her that I didn't hate her and tried to explain my need to connect with my roots, she simply couldn't understand. She reacted badly, refusing to speak to me for weeks, hanging up the telephone when I called. We never discussed that subject again.

My relationship with my parents had been difficult and rocky, something I always attributed to the fact that I was adopted. I'm not so sure that was the reason—or the sole reason; I think it was simply a case of personalities, inadequate and inappropriate child-rearing skills, and family dynamics, as in any family.

I have visited the area of my birth mother's home and the cemetery where her family members are buried. I discovered that I was originally named after her mother and her grandmother, names I carried until the time of my adoption. Then I was given a new name, a new identity, a new home, a new family, in a new community with a new culture. That must have been such a huge adjustment for a little two-year-old to make—an adjustment that would take me a lifetime to sort out and, in that sorting out, affect who I am today.

Kayla with her baby daughter.

Kayla Greenspan:
Mind games

When I began to collect stories for this book, a logical first step would have been to make a list of all the people I knew personally who were adopted or who had adopted children. Interestingly, I didn't do that at all. From the very beginning, the stories just seemed to find me; I simply told people about my project and the stories flooded in. There were times when it seemed to me that almost everyone must be adopted!

While visiting my sister in Toronto, we were invited to the home of childhood friends for dinner. I had been in touch with them over the years and knew their children (both of whom were adopted) but for some reason hadn't thought of them when compiling stories. That evening, I told them about the book I was writing and later on I realized that I should have asked if either of them would like to participate.

I contacted both Kayla and her brother by email and offered them the opportunity to share their stories. Kayla was eager to do so, but Dan didn't respond. I later learned from him that he really doesn't have "a story" because, unlike Kayla, he is not interested in seeking his biological family. He is quite content to live the life he has been given with the family he considers his "real" family.

Kayla and I agreed to get together the next time I was in Toronto. Her story is a work in progress, but she was very open and willing to share.

Kayla's Story

Kayla is a striking young woman—tall, blonde, and with the graceful body of a dancer, which she was. She is a teacher, a newlywed, and has just moved into a beautiful new home. She has been given every opportunity to pursue her interests and education, and lives a seemingly charmed life. She has a close and loving relationship with her brother and parents; and yet, she cries easily and often during our conversation about her search for her biological family.

"My parents told me I was adopted when I was very young, but I really understood what it meant when I was five and a half and we picked up my brother. I remember walking down the hall and into a room and I knew I didn't watch my mother's stomach getting bigger," said Kayla. The siblings are both very tall and very blond, in a large extended family of people who look completely different. Their parents are short and dark, as are most of the relatives. "We liked being different; my grandmother especially made me feel extra special," said Kayla. Since she and her brother look so much alike, there was never really any question about their relationship and they have always felt like a "team."

"I was happy, but I always wondered who my birth family was. In adolescence, I really started to think about it. At sixteen, I remember being in Florida with my grandparents and we were watching a program about adoption and a girl was given a letter from her birth mother. I asked my parents if there was a letter for me."

There was, in fact, a letter, but Kayla's parents didn't give it to her until she turned eighteen. At that age, she was legally able to register with the adoption disclosure registry and would, hopefully, be emotionally mature enough to deal with whatever her search might find.

"The letter was addressed to 'Shayna,' and my parents kept that as my middle name. The letter was written two days before I was given up. It said she [my birth mother] wanted me to know that she loved me and was giving me up because she and my birth father did not love each other and she couldn't keep me."

"I went to the adoption disclosure registry within two weeks. I put the form in and waited. I thought it would take years to hear anything. I went to camp that summer and came home for a day off and found a package on my bed. Within six months, we had been matched."

Finding a match is only the beginning of the next phase of the story. Kayla contacted a social worker who explained what the next steps would be and guided her through the process. Although excited to have the information, Kayla was not quite ready for a meeting. There was so much happening in her life, all of it exciting and happy. She was at university, living in residence, dating the boy who would become her husband. She wanted to take things very slowly with her new-found birth mother.

"I was starting university at the time and I just wanted to start communicating through letters. I got my first letter on my nineteenth birthday. The letter said, 'Wow, birthday girl! Wishing you the best.' She sent me a ring mounted with a Norwegian stone and wrote, 'May this guide you to me.'"

Kayla's birth mother is Norwegian, which explains her blonde hair. She was excited to find a missing piece of her puzzle.

"I wore the ring for a while. For about two years, we corresponded, and things went well. At twenty-one, I decided to send her a picture of myself. I never heard back. I took it pretty badly." At this point in the story, although it is years later, tears are streaming down Kayla's face.

The initial excitement turned to sadness and a sense of having been abandoned for a second time. Four long years passed before Kayla heard from her birth mother again, years in which she graduated from university, travelled, and decided to enrol in teachers' college. With her life once again back on track, Kayla received another email, "out of the blue."

This time, her birth mother invited Kayla to visit her and her family (she was married with two young children) and even offered to pay for the plane ticket. The tone was demanding, and Kayla says she was made to feel guilty if she refused the offer. "I feel like I'm a character in a movie I have never seen," she said. Too upset to even reply, Kayla tried to gather her thoughts and keep her emotions in check. Now that she had made contact, Kayla's birth mother began to pressure her, even to harass her by email. "She was attacking me, asking how I dared not reply."

Once again, Kayla did not respond, fearing further involvement with a woman who was making her uneasy. Then, something very strange: "She sent me a link to a breast cancer website. I asked my parents to come over and be with me when I opened it. I assumed that something happened in her family that she wanted to warn me about, but there was no message or explanation. She could have at least written one line!" That email left Kayla reeling, wondering what this woman wanted from her.

"She has been very persistent. Almost ten years later, she is still sending emails. I do want to meet her, but I just want to sit down with her, not with twenty-five of her relatives," says Kayla. Although it would be easier and more comfortable for Kayla if her birth mother would come to meet her so that Kayla could be in her comfort zone with the emotional support of her husband and family, her birth mother has so far refused, insisting instead that Kayla travel to meet her. At this point, it is not about to happen, but things may change when she finds out that she is a grandmother.

Kayla and Brian are now the proud parents of a beautiful little daughter of their own.

"I went into labour nine days early and I was out for dinner at a restaurant with Brian's colleagues when it all started. My labour was smooth and my delivery was quick. I don't remember details because everything happened so fast, but what I do remember was amazing! They put Sadie on my chest the second she was born. We bonded instantly. I am in love.

"I can't really describe how I feel being a mom and looking at my first blood relative. I think I'm still in shock. Everyone who meets her says she looks like Brian, but has my lips . . . she is so delicious!

"This has made me think about my birth mother more, especially having a girl. I think about what she must have felt the second I was born. I think about the fact that she must have held me before giving me up and how it felt to hold me because now I understand how precious it feels. It is the best feeling! I am reconsidering contacting her when things settle down here. I do want to let her know about Sadie, but at the same time I don't want her to start pressuring me again to fly out to meet her. I would prefer her to come here to meet me. This is where my support network is, where my life is."

Janice:
Please leave me alone

Janice and I have known each other for several years. We were introduced by a mutual client and have formed a professional relationship that is mutually beneficial. We are in allied businesses and are often in a position to refer clients to each other. Over the years, we have come to know, like, and respect one another, occasionally meeting for coffee or lunch.

During one of our coffee "dates," I mentioned to Janice that I was writing a book of adoption stories, and, to my surprise, she volunteered to share her own story. Until that day, I had not been aware that Janice was adopted. She often spoke fondly of her parents, with whom she had a very close and loving relationship, but of course hadn't felt any reason to say they were her adoptive parents.

There was no time that day to discuss her personal life, but Janice suggested we meet again over a glass of wine when we had lots of time. In spite of our busy and often conflicting schedules, we finally found a time to get together. Although initially she was willing to tell me the story and use her real name, she did later ask me to use a pseudonym so that she could protect the feelings of her birth family. Janice is, therefore, not the real name of the woman in the following story.

Janice's Story

Janice was in her mid-forties when her father died. She and her husband were on a much-needed Caribbean holiday when they got the call and rushed home immediately. "I had to take care of all of the arrangements," she said. "I've always been the one in charge of everything in my family; the organizer." This was a particularly difficult task because she found it so hard to cope with her loss. "I've always been a daddy's girl," she said. And being a middle-aged, high-powered career woman didn't change that.

Adopted as an infant by a couple in small-town Ontario, Janice is the middle of three children. Her older brother, also adopted, was born on the same date two years earlier. After Janice, a baby girl was born to her parents, though her mother had been told she would never bear children.

The children are all very different, but the family is close, and Janice has always been the "glue" that holds them together. Being adopted is just a fact and has never influenced how she feels as part of the family.

"I was spoiled rotten. I had a perfect childhood, an amazing childhood," she says. The family was not wealthy, but they were comfortable. Her father worked and her mother stayed home with the children. "Our house was the house that all the kids came to. We had a pool. I was a very active, athletic child. I was into ballet, figure skating, gymnastics . . ."

Though Janice's brother never showed any interest in finding his birth family, Janice was always curious about hers. "My mother used to read me stories. The Bambi story really got to me. It was like I was a little Bambi and she was 'another' mother who came to take care of me." The curiosity was simply that; there was never a feeling that something was missing or that she was with the "wrong" parents.

"To me, a mother is not someone who bears a child. It is the person who cares for you." The same can be said for a father. "When I was little, I used to have leg cramps, and my father would rub my legs for hours on end," said Janice.

"I thank the good lord that my birth mother had me, or I

would not be here; but I know I would be a different person if she had brought me up. My mom and dad taught me that anything is possible and I could do anything I want, and I believed them. That is why I take the risks that I do and do what I need to do to get where I want to be, and have the strength to keep going. They were always behind me."

Janice's physical and emotional strength were tested when, in her thirties, she was diagnosed with breast cancer. The desire to know her medical history led to a search for her biological family. First stop, the Children's Aid Society (CAS), which held the confidential information. The first thing she learned was heartbreaking. The records indicated that Janice's birth father had been married to someone else, with a family of his own, and wanted nothing to do with this child; he had wanted her to be aborted.

After a lengthy, apparently exhaustive search, the CAS finally called to tell Janice that they had found her birth family. "They said that my birth mother had died, but that I had siblings, and they asked me if I would write a letter stating that they could release my information to these family members. I sent the letter to the CAS, and a telephone call was arranged with my birth brother. The call was very strange and upsetting. He was telling me stories that just didn't make sense; the information didn't match the "non-identifying information" on my CAS case file. To make matters worse, these people now had access to all of my personal information. They knew where I live, that I own a business, etc."

When Janice called the CAS to voice her concerns, she was told that they do not make mistakes. After only one day, however, she got a call saying that they had, in fact, made a mistake and given her information to the wrong people.

Within a week, another call came in saying they had found her birth mother (who was, apparently, alive after all!) and that Janice could have her contact information. Skeptical, she took the information and arranged to contact her birth mother by telephone.

The first call lasted for four hours and was very emotional. Other calls followed over the next few months, until finally

Janice felt ready to meet her birth mother in person. Throughout this whole period, Janice's adoptive mother was supportive and happy for her daughter, but things quickly changed when the prospect of a face-to-face meeting seemed imminent.

"My mom was devastated. She thought she had lost me. She was scared. She wanted to go with me, but I said no. I had to do it on my own," said Janice.

She flew out West and spent a few days with her birth mother's family (she had married and had another daughter). The visit was intense, but satisfying in many ways. "We chatted until the wee hours, and I had a lot of questions answered. I told her that she had done the right thing, that I have had a wonderful life."

Finally, Janice could see where her physical features came from (though people have always thought she resembles her adoptive mom). "I have her eyes, her knobby knees, a similar mouth," says Janice, "but our personalities are very different."

For Janice, the meeting was good; it was sufficient. It had answered her lingering questions and filled in the blanks in her life. That was enough for her and she was happy to return to her home, her family, and her busy life.

Unfortunately, her birth mother felt that the meeting was just the beginning of a new relationship. She and her daughter began calling Janice frequently. They emailed, wrote, and pressured her for more contact. They came to visit and overstayed their welcome. They were very demanding of her attention and pushed Janice to the point of wanting to cut off contact completely.

"They did without me for forty years. They have their family, and I have mine," said Janice. "I felt that I am the glue in my family; I don't need to be the glue in their family. They are virtually strangers to me.

"My mom was so worried about losing me to my birth mother, but she knows now that she has nothing to worry about. When I was ill, for six weeks straight my mom drove me every day for radiation treatments. SHE is my mom!"

Kristin Blackburn:
One big, happy family

Mike and I worked together in the life insurance business for several years and became quite good friends. When we first met, he was going through a difficult time personally, as his marriage had recently broken up, and he had an infant son who was the centre of his life.

One day, he told me he had just had a phone call from a female friend of his who had heard about his marital problems and wanted to get together. He and Kristin had been friends for some time but had lost touch during Mike's brief marriage. She had also had a brief, unsuccessful marriage and had a daughter about the same age as Mike's son.

As friends, they began to see one another and to help each other deal with their situations; their children played together and got along well, and the relationship was comfortable and comforting for all.

As time went on, their friendship blossomed into love. I met Kristin and liked her very much and was very happy for them all.

One evening, my then-teenage daughter and I had dinner with Mike and Kristin, and, knowing that my daughter was adopted, Kristin shared her personal story with us. Although it is now several years later, I certainly remembered her story and wanted to include it in this book so I called and asked to interview her. Fortunately, she was willing to participate and invited me over to get an "update."

Kristin's Story

As a young child, I decided that Prince Charles was my father. My story was that he had had an affair and had to get rid of me, so he put me up for adoption.

Although it was not a big deal in my family to be adopted—my grandmother was adopted, and my father's sister was adopted—I do recall being teased when I was young and I think I always felt there was something "missing" in my family.

By my early teens, I was a rebellious teenager and in hindsight I wonder if some of that was because I didn't feel a connection with my parents. Maybe it was a struggle about my identity . . . why do I look like this? Who do I look like?

My adoptive parents had a biological son who was born with a disability and died at a very young age. They were told that any other biological children would be at risk of the same condition, so they adopted my brother and then me. We had a pleasant, upper-middle-class upbringing, enjoying all the typical activities such as ballet, tennis, and Sundays at the country club. My father was in the Foreign Service, and we had postings abroad.

In spite of the outward trappings, I felt a certain emptiness. I really wanted to know my story, but I hesitated to ask my parents or even let them know I wanted the information.

When I was sixteen, I had to do a high school co-op placement and I wanted to do it at the Children's Aid Society (CAS) . . . I wanted to figure things out and thought this would be a good way to do it.

I asked a lot of questions when I was there and read what I could. There was no Internet then, so it wasn't so easy.

I do remember telling my mom then that I wanted to search for my birth family. Through my placement at the CAS, I had found out about the adoption registry and how it worked at that time. My mom was fine with that and even offered to help me fill out the forms. In fact, she told me that she had some information—she knew my original name! Apparently, a prescription had been left in the diaper bag by the foster parents who cared for me before my adoption and it had my full name on it.

I had a few sessions with a social worker at the CAS, who helped me complete the forms, made easier because I had my original name. Because of that, the search yielded results very quickly. Before long, I received a registered letter—the first registered letter I had ever received—telling me that a match had been made! From the moment I read the letter until the time of my reunion with my birth mother, I have absolutely no memory . . . I seem to have blocked it out. I can't remember working with the social worker, telling my mom, exchanging letters with my birth mother.

The next thing I do remember is the actual reunion. It took place at the CAS, and the social worker was there. I was wearing a red turtleneck sweater and black and white plaid pants and "big hair"—and the temperature was in the eighties! The social worker went down to get my mother, and I stayed in the room. My mother walked into the room; she was wearing a red sweater and black and white pants! We just looked at each other—what could we say?

I remember the feelings: Who is this stranger? Will I be rejected again? What will she think of me? Will I have all of my questions answered? What ARE my questions?

I had created a photo album of my life, which I shared with her, and she had brought pictures to show me. She cried, and I just felt overwhelmed by it all. She had kept a picture of me as a baby in her sock drawer all those years. So, she hadn't just abandoned me and forgotten about me, which was important to me.

For that first visit, my birth father did not come. My mother explained that he had been adopted himself, but not until he was a teenager, so he had many horrific years in foster homes. He was afraid of what my life might have been and was not able to cope with it.

So, what was the story? Well, I am NOT the daughter of Prince Charles. My birth parents were young, both in their first year of university, when my mother found out she was pregnant. They were both afraid to tell their parents and, since they were at a university out of town, they were able to hide the pregnancy. My mother went to stay at a "home" until July when I was born; she left the baby to be adopted and returned home . . . where she married my father the very next month!

I really struggled with the fact that they married so soon after giving me up. They went on with their lives, just as planned. My father became a doctor, they had three more children, they have had a wonderful life—money, family, love. Knowing all of this has been very difficult for me and I've dealt with feelings of sadness, regret, and anger. I'm a full sibling to the other three, so why wasn't I part of this big, happy family?

After our initial meeting, I met my siblings and other family members on my mother's side, all of whom were very warm and welcoming. Oddly enough, my father's family—his adoptive family— were not accepting at all and never wanted to meet me or have any communication with me at all. Feelings of rejection haunted me once again.

The first few years with my "new-found" family were good; we got together for family occasions, kept in touch regularly, and seemed to be building a relationship; but then it stopped. There has never been an outright rejection, but I don't feel I am really a part of the family. My adoptive mom became ill with cancer, and I refocused back on her. When she died, my world crumbled, and I withdrew from a lot of things, including my biological family.

Maybe it just ran its course. I haven't seen any of them for a couple of years, though I do keep in touch with one sister. My daughter and her daughter look very much alike—exactly like me!

Since I was a teenager and had my job placement at the CAS, I have always known that I wanted to work there and planned my career accordingly. I am now a social worker at the CAS and for several years I have presented my own story as part of the training for foster and adoptive parents.

I am happily married and have a wonderful teenage daughter of my own now. My life and career are fulfilling, and most of my questions have been answered.

Ellen Jones:
A family gathered[2]

I was in the locker room at the gym, changing from my workout clothes and rushing to get to the office. I heard a familiar voice calling my name and turned to see Marlene, an old friend and my former camp counsellor. We stopped to chat for a few minutes and to catch up on what had been happening in each of our lives. I mentioned that I was writing this book because Marlene is a social worker and I thought perhaps she would know of someone I could interview.

"Have I got a story for you," she said. It was not a client, but a friend and colleague she was thinking of. She said she would call her friend and ask for permission to put me in touch with her, which she did. I called Ellen and introduced myself, and within minutes, we felt like the best of friends. There was an instant rapport, and I looked forward to meeting her in person. She invited me to her home and sent me detailed directions—how did she know that I'm "directionally challenged?"

When I arrived at the door, I was greeted by Ellen's husband. In the few steps it took to get from the front door to the living room where Ellen was waiting, he and I also had "bonded." He was warm and friendly and, for some reason, told me right away that he is originally from the Maritimes, as am I. Needless to say, the interview began on a very good note, and really felt more like a pleasant afternoon among friends. We drank tea, talked about life "down home," and then I listened as Ellen told me the story of her life.

---

2   The names in this story have been changed.

At one point, as tears slid down her cheeks and she paused to collect herself, I asked Ellen if this was too difficult for her. I reminded her that I'm not a therapist and I didn't want to cause any pain or bring up any memories that she had not dealt with. She assured me that she has had plenty of therapy and is just fine; she was emotional, but is now in a very good place and really wanted to share her story with me—and with you, the readers.

Ellen's Story

Life is good for Ellen now—very good, in fact—but it wasn't always thus. First came a troubled childhood and tortured adolescence, a self-destructive young adulthood, and the long road to recovery.

Ellen knew she was adopted and as a child she felt she didn't really "belong" in her family. She didn't look like her parents or younger brother (her parents' biological son) and didn't seem to think like them, either. "It was a lonely journey a lot of the time where I felt quite alone and I didn't feel a sense of connection," she said.

She began to rebel, getting into trouble and experimenting with drugs; by the time she was fourteen, Ellen had dropped out of school and was using hard drugs. Her parents were confused, distraught, and didn't know how to handle her. "It was a horrible time for them, I am sure. We didn't really work through it together. I don't think they knew how," she said.

"My parents were good people, educated people. They had never even been around an alcoholic and certainly not drug users."

Although her parents tried their best to be supportive and to help Ellen, she withdrew and struck out on her own. "You want your parents to be proud of you, to be interested in you, and it really just wasn't that kind of a story at all, and I think I just had to remove myself from them."

Ellen is convinced that being adopted caused her youthful angst; she later discovered that there was a biological component to her addiction as well.

"The times I grew up in and the family I was in . . . nobody talked about adoption. I needed to know about it, about where I came from and who I was. I felt there was something wrong with me because I was adopted. It was something shameful that we all knew but didn't talk about. I really did not know who I was. I became emotionally stunted at about age twelve."

These feelings had started very early for Ellen. "I remember, clear as a bell, at the age of five standing in the playground and wondering, 'Who am I, really?'" For many years, she searched for the answer. Her decision to quit school, her descent into the life of hard-core drug use, her emotional emptiness and distancing of herself from her family made life a living hell. Miraculously, though, by her mid-thirties, she had had enough. "I really started to grow up in my thirties; before that, I was just surviving."

When Ellen felt she had hit rock bottom, she knew that something had to change. "I always had an instinct for survival and a strong will to live. I always believed that I would get out of all that—heroin addiction and alcoholism. I didn't see that as who I really was and I had a strong drive to get beyond that."

Ellen not only pulled herself out of the gutter, she went back to school, completing university and even a graduate degree in social work; by helping herself, she also equipped herself to help others. It wasn't easy and it wasn't quick, but once she decided that her life had to change, she stuck with it. Her parents had never completely given up hope or abandoned her, and she began to realize how much they loved her and to value their support. "Many of my friends and peers, many of them adopted, did not make it out, did not have families with love and support," she said.

"I started to have a wonderful relationship with my parents. It did take time. I started visiting them quite often and we moved forward. I started to appreciate them as individuals, to understand their lives, their backgrounds; things began to make more sense."

Ellen's decision to go to a Parent Finders meeting with a friend was a pivotal event in her road to recovery. For twelve years, she went to meetings and derived support from the people she met there. It was a long road, often frustrating, but she was determined to find her birth mother and to fill the void that she carried within her. The same strength of character that enabled her to conquer substance abuse and to persevere with her education provided her with the courage and determination to keep searching.

Eventually, the search bore fruit, though not the happy ending Ellen had long hoped for. Her birth mother had been fighting demons of her own. Both she and a brother she lived with and cared for were alcoholics. She had been separated from her husband when she became pregnant and gave birth to Ellen in her late twenties and had never told Ellen's birth father. She travelled across the country and had the child all alone in a strange city and under extremely difficult circumstances.

"She really tried to forget it had happened," said Ellen after meeting her birth mother. "I feel sorry that the story was what it was, for her and for me."

After a couple of unpleasant meetings, Ellen had had enough. "After the second visit, I was truly grateful that I didn't grow up with her," she said. "I saw her one more time; after that, our relationship broke down completely."

In spite of—or perhaps because of—the difficult reunion with her birth mother, Ellen continued her search for her birth father, who had never been told of her existence. She was able to find out who he was and attempted to contact him but he did not respond. Eventually she located his brother, who told her that her father was an alcoholic and a paranoid schizophrenic; the family had no idea where he was.

The next four years were a time of connecting with her birth father's family, who welcomed Ellen warmly. It was also during this time that she and Bill, who had known each other for some time, were developing their relationship. "Their [her birth father's family] love and acceptance for me had opened the floodgates for me. I already knew Bill, but we really connected once I felt that I was loveable."

Then Ellen's birth uncle found his brother. "We found him in a hospital with terminal cancer. We went to visit him. Bill brought cigars that said 'It's a Girl,' and we travelled to meet him at the hospital. For three years, I went once a month with my birth uncle to visit my father. Meeting me extended his life; he had a wonderful time."

Having found a level of peace in her personal life and graduated from university, in her mid-forties, Ellen decided to take the plunge and marry Bill. "We decided to invite everybody—adoptive family, birth family, relatives on both sides . . . I realized that this was my life and these are the people in my life and this is what it is. It was a wonderful time."

"Life is pretty good these days. I realize though that you don't get over some of these things. I feel grateful today. I needed so much for so many years that I was not even aware of the needs of others. Now that I am on the other side, I am at a place of giving back and just living."

Toby, Debra's birth mother, Debra, and her half-sister Sarna.

Debra Dressler:
A spiritual awakening

I must give credit once again to *The Canadian Jewish News* for being the source of a great lead for one of my adoption stories. Although the focus of the article was the introduction of a new female rabbi who had recently arrived in London, Ontario, it did mention the unusual fact that this rabbi had not been born Jewish. Her journey from a childhood in small-town USA, where she didn't even know anyone Jewish, to become a spiritual leader of a Canadian Jewish congregation is a very interesting human interest story. The part that grabbed my attention was the fact that she had been adopted—which, in my opinion, added another layer of intrigue.

As soon as I finished reading the article, I called the newspaper and spoke to my colleague who had written it. I asked if she would be good enough to contact Rabbi Dressler and ask for permission for me to call her.

My first conversation with Rabbi Dressler was pleasant and easy, and she readily agreed to participate in my book. We exchanged a few emails and then arranged for another, more in-depth telephone conversation once she had had an opportunity to settle into her new city and job. As we began the interview, she told me that she was happy I had called her. She felt that the timing was right for her to share her story and she welcomed the chance to do so. I'm sure that my readers will be just as glad as I am that she felt willing to let us into her life and to learn how she was able to answer the question, "Who am I, really?"

Debra's Story

There was never a time that Debra was unaware of being adopted; it was just a fact of life, taken for granted by her and everyone she knew. Although both her older brother and younger sister are the biological children of her parents, Debra says that other family members on her mother's side were also adopted, so there was never any stigma attached to it.

"I was always very different from the rest of my family, but I had friends who felt that they didn't belong in their families, either, although they shared their families' DNA."

Growing up in a suburb of Lansing, Michigan, in what she describes as a "secular, Christian family—we celebrated Christmas and Easter but did not go to church," Debra said her contacts with "the Jewish world" were very limited. "I had an attraction to *Fiddler on the Roof* and identified with the story of Anne Frank," but didn't really know why.

When Debra began her university studies at the Wharton School, she had, for the first time, Jewish friends and colleagues. Ironically, most of them assumed that Debra was Jewish as well. "My maiden name is 'Stahlberg,' and I 'look' Jewish, so my friends thought I was." Adding to the irony is the fact that the name Stahlberg is German, but definitely not Jewish. "My father is German. His older half-brothers were both German soldiers, and his father was a member of the Nazi party—a very interesting pedigree for someone who is now a rabbi!"

For some reason then unknown, Debra felt a strong pull toward anything Jewish. "At university, when the place would empty out at Rosh Hashana and Yom Kippur, I always had the feeling that I was supposed to be somewhere, a feeling I did not have with Christianity."

In tandem with Debra's search for a spiritual home, she began to search for her biological roots as well, mainly in a quest for medical information. "I knew that I would like to marry and have children someday and I knew that I wanted to find my birth family because of that. I was aware that my biological grandmother had cancer at a young age and I wanted more medical information.

"In Michigan, when I was born, the only way to get information was if both parties had signed a release. I did the circuit of adoption support groups. I found a judge who was sympathetic and was willing to give [one's] file to a third party, who would track down the other party and ask them to sign the release. She did that for me and found that my birth mother was from Chicago. She had been a student at Michigan State University when I was born and had stayed there."

Debra's birth mother signed the release, clearing the way for the adoption agency to share information with Debra. "I read through about eight pages of information. At the end of one paragraph, it said 'the mother was of the Jewish faith.' It was the best news I had ever gotten! It might have been upsetting, or completely irrelevant, to someone else." But for Debra, the news signalled the beginning of her journey "back" to Judaism.

"I started taking Judaism courses at the university and through a local congregation. I kept taking more classes, always wanting to know more. I felt like a convert, although I am not. [The Jewish religion is matrilineal; having been born to a Jewish mother, Debra is considered to be Jewish by birth.] To complete my learning in a formal way, I went through the conversion process and had a bat mitzvah and, along the way, I got this crazy idea that I wanted to become a rabbi."

She was encouraged, in a "back-handed" kind of way, by her rabbi. He had told her, "I look at you and I see leadership. I see a president of the congregation." Debra's reply was that she was flattered, but she wanted HIS job!

The goal was daunting for a number of reasons. Academically, it was a challenge to meet the entrance requirements to Hebrew Union College, the institution that trains Reform rabbis. Debra's undergraduate studies had been in business rather than liberal arts, and she was missing some prerequisites to qualify her for graduate-level studies. In addition, she had not grown up Jewish and was therefore missing many important life experiences that would prepare her to work as a rabbi.

"I was asked to get involved with the youth group, to take some graduate-level courses, and to take adult study courses through the Reform movement," she said. She also made use of her administrative background by working as the assistant executive director of a congregation, which both enabled her to earn a living and also provided an informal education in the workings of a Jewish community. "It was a way to be even closer to my goal," she said.

"In the year 2000, I was accepted to Hebrew Union College. At that point, I was divorced [her first husband was not Jewish but was supportive of her return to Judaism] and I took my seven-year-old daughter to Israel for a year. It was a fantastic experience for both of us."

Throughout her journey, Debra's adoptive family supported her unconditionally. "My family was perfectly happy that I found Judaism . . . it was a bit difficult that their grandchildren would not be celebrating Christmas with them, but they got over it," she said.

"When we went to Israel, my mother went with us for a few weeks and helped us get settled. Without my mother's help, I could never have accomplished what I did," said Debra. It was particularly meaningful for them to spend that time together, as her mother passed away later that year.

Ironically, it was Debra's birth mother who was not thrilled with her decision to become a rabbi.

Although she had grown up in a Jewish family, she had "issues" with the organized Jewish community.

Following Debra's search, and some initial communication, they had met in 1990, at a restaurant in Detroit. "We just looked at each other, in a way that you don't look at anyone else. I had never looked like anyone and I look a lot like her."

There were many similarities and coincidences. "I was a super-gifted, advanced child, and there weren't any other kids like me [in the adoptive family]," said Debra. "It was the same with Judaism. I found, through my biological heritage, a spiritual home that I could never find anywhere else."

When her birth mother and adoptive family met, there was instant rapport. "They hit it off immediately. Both my adoptive mother and my birth mother were teaching at the same community college!" They knew many of the same people, yet had never guessed that they had a daughter in common!

For a number of years, Debra and her birth mother enjoyed a close relationship, but that is no longer the case. Debra has moved on with her "new" life and career. Her second marriage, in which she gave birth to two more daughters, has ended, but she has found immeasurable fulfillment in her role as a congregational rabbi and as the mother to three wonderful daughters.

Her quest to find out who she "really" is has had a most satisfying conclusion.

David Calder.

David Calder:
Olympic champion

I routinely read the local newspaper every morning and I just as routinely remove the sports section before I begin. I don't know why I do this, I just do. I really don't have any interest in sports, so it makes it easier to simply get rid of that section.

One morning, I found myself deeply engrossed in a story about a silver medal that two Canadian rowers had just won in the summer Olympics. I have no idea why I was even reading the story and certainly don't know why I read it from beginning to end; but I did, and I was greatly rewarded for doing so. I discovered that one of the men had been adopted. I was anxious to meet him and hear his story.

It took some detective work to finally connect with Dave Calder, because, to my surprise, there are two people by the same name in the same small town, and apparently they are not even related. I first contacted the wrong one, who was unable to help me find the correct one. Eventually, I did finally reach Dave by telephone at his office. He said he was tired because he had been travelling, and there was a time change, and he would rather I called again in a few days. He had, unfortunately, been in Ottawa, where I live; if I had reached him the week before, we could probably have met in person while he was here.

I persisted and did manage to have a nice chat with Dave, soon after the initial call. I arranged to meet him when I next travelled to Victoria, and, since that first meeting, we have had several others. I have grown very fond of him and feel a strong connection with him. I even follow his rowing progress on his website and blog.

Dave's Story

My life has always been blessed. I have two loving parents who raised my three older sisters and me with love and provided well for us. At times, my mom's unconditional love had to sneak in to soothe me with warmth after the sting of my dad's tendency toward tough love had hit. Hindsight, being what it is, has made me see that my mom's love made me the gentle, loving husband and father I am today, while my dad's love turned me into the driven, pragmatic Olympic medalist I've worked so hard to become. At the age of thirty-three, and as a happily married parent of two children, I understand the importance of both approaches working together.

But I had parents—of sorts—before my parents. Before a lot of things. Before my memory, which is so abstract for children, especially when they try to remember significant events. My point of discovery came one day while I was driving with my mom and the little girl—Melissa—she used to babysit. It was a sunny day, but much of the sun's light was blocked by the densely forested road we were driving down. Sitting in the back seat, Melissa innocently told me that my mom wasn't my real Mom. Well, of course my mom is my real mom, I thought. My little brain didn't know what that meant, but I immediately denied it. Looking to my mom for support, I was completely thrown off when her response came back: "We'll talk about this when we get home."

It turned out I was adopted. It took years to finally ask my mom about it. Guilt had stopped me. Why should I be curious? I had everything I could ever need. Like I said, my life was blessed. My mom took me into her room and closed the door behind us—I had never been in my parents' room with the door closed. She knelt in front of the window bench and opened a trunk hidden beneath it. Very carefully, she pulled out a small box the size of a photo album, but no thicker than half an inch, and handed it to me: "This is all that I know. I'm sorry; I wish I could tell you more."

For years, I had two concrete details linking me to my birth family: (1) my city of birth, and (2) the fact that my maternal grandparents were welders. There is little the average person can do with such scarce information.

When I was nineteen and had a degree of autonomy from my parents, I decided to write the provincial agency responsible for adoptions and request information on formal steps toward a reunion. Thankfully, this was a slow process—and a year later, I withdrew my application. As a twenty-one-year-old, I had qualified to race for Canada at the 2000 Sydney Olympic Games as a rower. The thought of a poorly timed reunification, or the potential baggage of a distraught birth mother, scared me off. It was not my time to search.

Disappointingly, I finished seventh in Sydney. Devastated by the result, my parents and three sisters—all there in Sydney—swooped in to save me. During the closing ceremonies, I was with all 10,000 athletes in the centre of the Olympic Stadium when I witnessed the official Olympic flag being passed from the mayor of Sydney to the mayor of Athens. I knew then that my dream of winning at the Olympics was not tied to a city, but to sport. It would take another four years of commitment, but I knew I would get another chance in Athens.

I set myself to work. I pushed as hard as I could in training that next year. It was paying off—once again, I was a leader on the team. My body was paying the price: I was sore, and that soreness was building, but I wasn't ready for what happened. The day before we left for the 2001 World Championships I could not get out of bed to get to practice. I writhed in pain. The team doctor told me later that day that he had never seen two herniated disks in a person's spine so severely gone. He had already set up a meeting with the leading surgeon.

There were rowers I knew who had seen unsuccessful results from surgery on their backs, and I decided that I would take the time to heal. I didn't know I would need a year. So what did I do? I jumped into my gas-guzzling '89 black softtop jeep and started to drive east from Victoria. Depending on who asked, I had a variety of destinations. The woman of my dreams had relocated to Montreal to study at McGill—I was definitely heading to Montreal. My parents had split, and my dad was living in Regina. While I was camped out there, waiting for my student-loan payment to be deposited into my bank account, the unimaginable events of 9/11 happened. My best friend's first day of his new job across the street from Tower 1 in New York City was September 11. I was also definitely heading to New York. All this, however, was a cover for a covert trip to Brandon, Manitoba. I only told one person what I was doing.

I found the cheapest motel I could, ripped out the "W" page from the yellow pages containing the names and addresses of welders in the area surrounding Brandon, and started my search. I methodically located each welder's shop on a map I had purchased at the Petro-Canada and planned my route. It took only one shop to realize my approach was flawed, but I kept going.

"Excuse me, sir, my name is Dave and I'm looking for my birth mom. She gave me up in 1978 when she was nineteen, so that would make her forty-two. All I know is that I was born in the Brandon hospital and that her parents were welders. Do you think you might know of anyone who could fit that description?"

To a man, everyone I asked initially thought they knew someone who could fit that description. Phone calls were made. Ages were checked. Questions were asked. Inevitably, no one fit that description. The experience was exhausting.

After the Olympics, I had gone bungee jumping in Australia. I bought the all-day pass—it was cheaper. The first jump was exhilarating and full of unexpected excitement, the unknown possibilities. By the fifth and sixth jumps, I just wanted to go home. My search through the Brandon welding community brought back similar sentiments.

My seventh and sworn last cold-call of the day was an exception to the rest. The man behind the counter immediately answered "No. But—" he added, "I think you should head over to the Children and Family Services office. My wife's a social worker there." Although he was sympathetic to my cause, he certainly did not approve of my approach.

When I arrived at the Ministry office, I was directed to the waiting area. From what I could gather, there were two social workers, both women, working out of two separate offices. The welder's wife was busy with a client, her door closed. The second office door was open, and as the social worker finished her phone call she turned and looked at me. She just stared. After what felt like an eternity of awkward silence, she motioned for me to come in and have a seat in her office. We both sat, each on our own side of her desk, in silence, her stare trying to tell me something.

Finally, I had to break the silence. "Hello, my name is Dave and I'm looking for—"

I was cut off. "I know who you are, Dave," the social worker said as tears filled her eyes, "and I know what you're looking for. My name is Lynn—it is very nice to see you after all these years."

Lynn got up out of her chair and opened a large drawer from her filing cabinet. Her fingers lightly trickled over the various files as if she were playing a harp. Finally, she stopped at a particular file, looked at it in its place, then, as if looking around the room to ensure no one was looking, she pulled the file out of the cabinet drawer. "Everything you are looking for is right here in this file. I legally can't tell you anything that's in it yet. I can tell you that parts of your story will be difficult to learn, but, in the end, you will have a happy reunion. Can you give me two weeks?"

With that, Lynn had me sign my end of a reunification consent form, and I was sent off. I continued my pilgrimage east. When I was about thirty kilometres out of Brandon, I swerved onto the gravel shoulder and slammed on the brakes. I pulled out my maps and spread them across the hood of my jeep. Then I called Rachel—the woman of my dreams waiting in Montreal—and in tears asked for guidance.

A huge portion of my adopted family live in Winnipeg, and I needed to be somewhere familiar. My mom's youngest brother, Mike, has always had great perspective on big issues. I spent a few days decompressing with him and my extended family. Yet, I was being drawn farther east to Montreal where I knew Rachel was establishing herself. I wanted to be significant to her; I wanted her to be part of my adoption story, too.

En route, I managed to find myself in the autumn wilderness of Northern Ontario and Quebec. For a stretch of what felt like a month (and amounted to five days), I camped alone with my thoughts. Upon arrival in Montreal, the spark quickly lit the fire again for Rachel and me. I knew right then I wanted to be with her for the rest of my life.

My best friend, Morgan, was still settling himself in New York City, with the chaos and trauma of being smack in the middle of the September 11 attacks; I wanted desperately to see him and to know that he was okay. True to form, he stoically marched on but was noticeably impacted by what he witnessed in the streets that day.

My eldest sister's wedding was my deadline to be back in Victoria. By the time I got back to Montreal, Rachel, also impacted by the terrorist attacks, was certain I shouldn't fly anywhere. It was impossible to say goodbye, and, as a result, when I finally got back into the Jeep to head home, I had to drive fast. I didn't stop for more than a few hours in any one spot all the way back. The day I cruised through the snow-covered Rocky Mountains heading for the coast, my phone lost reception for most of the day. I had to push hard to make the last ferry of the day, so I didn't stop to check messages until I got in line.

"One new message. Message one: "Hello, David, it's Lynn from Brandon. I have great news. Can you come into my office in the next day or so? This is my last week before I retire, and I can't wait to tie all the pieces together for you."

I called Lynn the next morning from my mom's house, where my family was busily preparing for my sister's wedding. Secretly, in my bedroom, I learned most of the answers to the questions I knew to ask. My birth mom, Donna, was nineteen when she had me. Her mom forced her to put me up for adoption. The story for folks in their small community was that Donna was having a cancerous tumour removed. Me.

My birth mom married her boyfriend, Garth, a different man than my birth father, a year after I was born. The two dated while Donna was pregnant with me. They had three sons together—my three half-brothers. Lynn was telling me all these details and I was just scribbling them down as if I'd have a quiz on it later. Then Lynn paused. She took a deep breath before saying: "The day we met, I told you that it would be difficult to learn the whole story of your birth mother. Well, David, Donna died in 1988." Tragically, when my youngest half-brother was six months old, Donna fell into a coma while she was having her wisdom teeth removed. She was in a coma for four years before she died from complications, having caught pneumonia.

Donna was twenty-eight when she died; I was nine.

Lynn went on to tell me her connection to the family. This is where the universe had conspired to help me. She was Donna's social worker in 1978 when I was given up for adoption. Years later, when Donna fell into her coma, Lynn and my birth family shared a back fence. She was their social worker over the four years Donna was in her coma; and then their grief counsellor when she eventually died. No one else could have connected the dots for me, no one else knew the story, the whole story, and somehow I arrived on Lynn's office doorstep three weeks ahead of her retirement. I was meant to find my birth family.

My sister's wedding was beautifully set with the crashing waves of the West Coast as a backdrop. After the wedding was over, and while my family was still all gathered in one city, I was able to share the details of my adventure to Brandon with them. As the youngest in my family, and having only sisters, three of them, I often found myself hogging the spotlight. The Olympic Games helped with that a bit, as did a very loving and supportive grandfather. I knew that I didn't want to take any attention from my sister. Overwhelmingly, they were all happy for me, and each in their own way very interested in the story that was partially theirs.

Lynn set up a phone call for me with Garth. In preparing me for the call, she told me how she had bent the provincial rules a little to expedite the reunification process so as to meet her retirement timeline. "The form you filled out in my office allowed me to search the database to see if your birth family had registered a reunification consent form with the province." She hesitated, "I knew there would've been a ton of red tape to cut through, and I would have retired before I heard back from the central office; so I called Garth directly, because no one had registered." We both laughed nervously a little before she added "They knew about you. They all knew about you. They've all always known about you."

Garth had been open about Donna's pregnancy and adoption with the three boys their whole lives. After Donna died, I think the idea of an adopted brother became a living extension of their mother. When I was born, Donna named me Christopher, so that's how they had always thought of their adopted brother. Lynn explained that one of the three boys had to be the one to register, because Garth technically was not related to me.

Over the month of November, Garth, my three half-brothers, and I spoke on the phone fairly regularly. Over the first few conversations, I discovered my maternal grandparents were still alive—both battling different forms of cancer. I found out about Donna's grad year—the year she had me. I found out about her relationship with Garth. I found out all the bits that were easy to answer, but then I wanted to find out about my birth father. The answers dried up.

I knew that I wanted to connect with my birth father on the same trip to Manitoba I was taking to meet Garth and my half-brothers. It became clear very quickly that Garth had no intention of telling me anything about him. It seemed to me that Garth was just getting used to having me to himself—maybe he felt that I had brought back a connection to Donna. He didn't want to share that connection with the guy who had knocked up the love of his life.

Donna's best friend in high school supported her through her pregnancy and my adoption. Garth gave me her contact information, knowing that she would want to talk to me twenty-one years after the adoption. Garth had obviously already spoken with her and had asked her not to share any information about my birth father with me.

My strategy was simply to bombard her with as many questions about my birth father as possible. I figured she'd slip back into that time and start speaking to my questions without her filter on. In all her stories and remembrances, there was never a malicious word spoken about my birth father. Her stories burst with young, exciting, and irrational memories.

After talking for over an hour, the name "Tony" slipped out. As soon as that happened, both our voices froze. There was a moment of careful calculation from her end of the line that I swear I heard. She knew that it was my right to know my birth father's name. She knew that Donna would've wanted me to know. All she had to do was give me Anthony's last name—and she did.

Garth and I arranged a reunion for December in Manitoba. Lynn had retired to British Columbia, so I needed neutral support for when I went to meet my birth mother's family. I didn't want to be worried about whoever came with me and how the reunion was impacting him or her. I wanted to be present—to pay attention to my emotions. Both my parents offered to come with me. They had separated a few years before and weren't talking to each other. In so many ways, I wanted both of them to come, but that was impossible.

In my preparation for the trip I wanted to connect with Anthony. I sent him a letter that stated who I was and that I was coming to town. I agonized over this letter. It was handwritten. Line by line, I chose each word carefully. I offered that I wanted to meet him. My concern was that he would be dismissive. In the letter, I provided my email address for him to reply quickly to my letter. I suggested that if I hadn't heard from him by the time I left for Virden, I would likely show up on his doorstep now that I had his address.

I felt like my mom was scared of losing me. It might not be true, but I felt like there was nothing I could say that would make her feel any more comfortable with the idea—except to go through with it and come home, showing that nothing changed. So that's what I did. I spoke less and less of the details around my mom as the date came closer, and tried to just slip away for the three-day trip.

My dad, on the other hand, thought that it would be fun to make a boys' road trip out of it. He was living in Regina with his partner and explained that it was only a few hours' drive from their place. I considered his proposition for a long time, but came back to the idea that I wanted to keep the experience to myself.

I invited Rachel. I knew what I was doing; I wanted her in my life forever. We were dating long-distance and it was getting hard. It was a calculated risk, but I knew that this experience would forge a bond that would become a pillar of our relationship. It didn't hurt that she was studying to become a social worker at McGill, so when I was questioned about my choice, I simply explained that she had the practical skills to support me through the reunion.

To my surprise, I got an email from Anthony fairly quickly—about a week after I sent the letter. In his note, he wrote that he was never told about me and that he would be interested in a meeting. I arranged to meet him on my way into town at a coffee shop. Donna's side of the family didn't know anything about my arrangements.

Both Rachel and I flew into Winnipeg; I was coming from Victoria, and she was coming from Montreal. My uncle lent us his family's minivan and we started the drive out to Virden, Manitoba. Although my birth family offered to put us up, I felt it was important to have a separate space to decompress each night. As we approached Virden, I remember asking Rachel if she wanted to just keep driving; I'm not sure if she knew if I was kidding or not—I'm not sure if I knew if I was kidding or not.

We parked and got out of the van. As we walked around the building to the front door, I peeked through the windows. I saw the only couple in the shop. My heart was in my throat. We walked in and said our hellos. We sat down. For a moment, it felt as if two leaders were meeting on a battlefield, each with his trusted lieutenant at his side: Rachel at mine, and Anthony's wife of many years, Maureen, at his. My letter to Anthony was her first warning of a child from a long-ago-forgotten—not to mention dead—high school sweetheart. I could tell she did not believe I was his son.

A few seconds ticked by in silence. It felt as if time stopped. Just before awkwardness set in, Anthony spoke: "I didn't know that Donna had a baby. I thought, maybe—but when I asked around, I was told no." He looked at me, in my eyes, and then he stared at my hands, folded on the table in front of me. Our hands were identical. "Looking at you—you *are* mine. It has to be true." My protective wall crumbled. I snuck my hand under the table and clutched Rachel's for external protection. In my numbness, Rachel carried the conversation for a time.

Once I regained my bearings, I pulled out a photo album I had put together for Donna's family. The pictures were copies of significant moments in my life, at a sampling of ages. I showed Anthony and Maureen the pictures. Maureen, still not wanting to believe I was Anthony's child, broke down for the first time. She produced a family picture of her three boys with Anthony. Looking through my album was like looking at her three boys—there was no doubt now.

My questions turned to Anthony's relationship with Donna. The way that Anthony spoke about Donna was so passionate, tender, and loving that Maureen had to excuse herself from the coffee shop. He went on at length about the true love and magic he felt around Donna. She started to push him away, and he didn't know why—until now.

In planning the coffee meeting with Anthony, I had built in a one-hour safety. We had to be on our way after an hour in order to make it to Donna's family in time. One hour was not enough, but it was safe. We climbed back into the minivan, and I just started to drive. I got three blocks away and pulled over and just started sobbing. I was so exhausted that all I wanted to do was check into the hotel for the night.

When we drove into the driveway at Garth's house, we were welcomed by an overwhelming number of people. Garth, my three half-brothers, Garth's wife, and their two girls. Later, Donna's brother and son arrived, and Donna's parents arrived. At one point, I remember the heads of the neighbour's kids popping in the door and yelling, "We just wanted to see him!" and disappearing as fast as they came.

Within an hour, it felt as if we'd all known each other our entire lives, or that we had all been waiting for that day to arrive. We stayed up long into the night swapping stories—comparing what we were doing at the same time over the years, only in our separate corners of Canada.

The next morning, Rachel and I woke up and went to the cemetery where Donna was buried. My whole life, I felt a connection to the abstract thought of my birth mother—but for the majority of my life she had been dead. Maybe that's why I felt that connection? Maybe her death gave her the freedom to supernaturally be present in my life. My search was always for Donna. I didn't ever think about siblings or even my birth father—it was always her.

I remember standing over her grave and feeling a wave of emotion crash over me. When Lynn explained to me in that initial phone conversation that Donna had died years before, it was all so factual, black and white. There was a uselessness to emotion because of the everlasting effects of death, spilt milk, and all. In that moment when I could see the dirt covering her body, the headstone marking her eternal bed, she became human for the first time for me. I started to cry.

There she was—I had found her—but I couldn't get any closer to her. I fell to my knees and cried over her grave. I wanted to talk to her. I wanted her answers—not Garth's, not Anthony's, not Donna's girlfriend's, parents', or sons'.

It was ironic that until I was standing over Donna's grave, I didn't realize that she was the one thing I was looking for. In searching for her, I have extended my family but, as promised to my mother, nothing has changed. I am who I am because of my fortunate upbringing. My life is now enriched by the events and people that came before—and led to—that upbringing.

Mike with his mother and daughter.

Mike Magee:
My mother's a star!

I've done some freelance writing for a local community newspaper and, from time to time, I drop in to chat with the editor, Michael. On one such occasion, I told him about my book and asked if he knew of anyone who might be a good subject for an interview. He said he'd give it some thought and let me know.

Within a day or two, I received an email with the names and contact information for two possible adoption stories, both of which sounded intriguing. The first one didn't pan out, but the second one led me to a website for Shari Ullrich, a well-known West Coast musician. I decided to call rather than email and was happy to be able to reach her easily. She was very friendly and happy to talk to me. I quickly discovered that I had made two erroneous assumptions: I assumed that Shari was the adoptee, but she is, in fact, the birth mother who had given up her child for adoption. I had also assumed that the person who suggested I call her was a friend of hers; but she had never heard of him and had no idea who he was! (I subsequently learned that he knew her story because he is also a music writer, is a fan of her music, and knew her personal story through her music and website.)

Shari told me she would contact her son and ask him if I could get in touch with him. Fortunately for me, he was more than willing to speak to me. We had a long conversation, an instant rapport across the phone line and across the continent, and he agreed to take part in my project.

I asked Mike to begin by emailing me a brief outline of his story; I asked a few basic questions and told him he could even do it in point form. I would then get back in touch with him to do a more thorough interview and we would proceed from there. He agreed.

I waited and waited and, after a couple of "gentle reminders," Mike did send me an email. It was not in point form. It was not brief. It was not the basis of an in-depth interview. It was, as you will see, his story—told with such raw emotion that I was sitting at my computer sobbing. When I finished reading it, I called him and said, "It's perfect—I'm crying my eyes out!" I want to present Mike's story exactly as told by him.

Mike's Story

My wife, Ann, received the first email. It was morning, sometime in July 2007, and we had an old friend over for the weekend. He and I were having coffee and talking when Ann called me into the room we called the "office."

"Mike, you need to sit down and read this," was all she said. I read the message she had open on the computer screen. The body of the message consisted only of the following: "Ann—my apologies for misspelling your name. Shari." This made no sense. Who is Shari? I don't know a Shari. And when did she misspell Ann's name? Then I looked at the subject line. It read: "RE: Contact from Michael's Birth Mother."

I was momentarily numb. My next thought was that it must be a joke, that someone got hold of a list from a public agency somewhere and was spamming the names on it. Then Ann showed me the web page she had opened, the one that she had pulled from the email address. There was a picture. And a bio. I read the bio, which put the woman whose picture smiled back at me at the exact place, San Rafael, California, and the exact year, 1967, to have given birth to me.

Now I looked hard at the picture. It took me a minute to grasp all of this, but my wife was way ahead of me. "That has to be her," she said, as we looked at the picture.

So, I replied cautiously to the cryptic message, pleading

that it not be a joke, and giving a few vital statistics to confirm that I might be the person this mysterious emailer was trying to reach. I pressed "send" and held my breath. Within a few minutes, another message came through: the one that I was supposed to have received but for some reason had never made it to us. This email explained who she was and why she was contacting Ann first; and it left no doubt that this person was my birth mother.

My birth mother. It seemed so impossible that ten minutes ago, I was having a cup of coffee with a friend talking about God only knows what, and now I was staring at an email message and a picture of my birth mother.

My birth mother.

Holy shit. My birth mother.

In her next message, she gave her phone number. I dialed the area code and the next six digits . . . then waited an eternity before I finally pressed the seventh. The phone rang, and a voice answered—a voice that sounded instantly familiar, warm, friendly, and as incredulous as I felt.

I was talking to my birth mother.

My birth mother! I always knew I was adopted. I don't recall ever knowing anything different. It was always talked about openly. It seemed so natural to me that I often wondered how strange it must have felt to other children to have been born to their actual parents. I mean, their parents had to keep them, whether they wanted to or not! But my parents *chose* me . . . they had their pick of any child they wanted, and *I* was their first choice. That felt special. And really, as life for me in Marin County, California, unfolded, there was a lot to be thankful for.

Although I'm sure that the nostalgia that comes with age puts a glossy shine on it, much of what gets forgotten over time is only the insignificant gripes of a privileged teenager living a privileged life. And by that I don't mean we lived extravagantly; but just that we lived well. My father owned (and still does) a successful heavy equipment business, and my mom stayed home. The neighborhood I grew up in was all much the same: lots of kids, fathers who all made a good living and came home to be with their families in the evening, and mothers who stayed home and all knew each other. We could round up a dozen kids to play a football game in the street in less than five minutes, and when the light started to fail, we would hear all the mothers calling us in to dinner. On the weekends, if I arrived home from a Little League game to an empty house, I could walk out to the front yard, hear which house everyone was gathered at for the evening, and go there and enter through the front door like it was my own home.

Looking back on it now, I suppose there were plenty of times when I might have wondered more about my true genetic heritage; but I never gave it much thought. My father and I are very different in many ways—ways that were a bit awkward at times. He is very much an extrovert and a driven, adventurous person. He needed to have a lot of people around and enjoyed being the centre of attention. Hence, it was more often than not that when I arrived home from one of those Little League games, it was our house that everyone was gathered at. On his side of the family, they were all like him, and I often felt shy around them. As I got older, I would come to fear the times that they would try to pull me out of my shell by trying to coax me into one kind of performance or another. But rather than ponder this difference as the result of not being genetically related, I just accepted that I was this way and they were that way, and never gave it a second thought.

No matter what else happened in our lives, I always felt incredibly loved, as much as I think it is possible for any child to feel loved, regardless of how parent and child came to be together. As I grew into adulthood, and questions about whether I was curious about who my "real" parents were came more frequently, I would reflect on this and think that the parents I had were as "real" as I could imagine parents to be. I had been given no reason or motivation in my life to think that anything more could be gained by opening a door that, for all I knew, protected me from some very potentially sad, scary, or, at the very least, emotionally charged truths. Not that I didn't wonder at times who out there in the world might have given birth to me; but really, I didn't wonder very often.

The story I was told was that my birth mother was a young

girl at the time, in high school, probably, and was simply too young to keep a child. I pictured her as I pictured my parents at that time in their lives, as young and beautiful as they were in their old photo albums. Actually, I pictured a young couple, never solely a woman, and imagined the relief they must have felt at being able to get out of this terrible jam they were in, having this baby at such a young age, and knowing that it was now in such a great home. (It didn't occur to me at that age that they would have had no knowledge of where I was placed.) I was happy for them that they could get on with their lives, as if that was the beginning and the end of their connection to me, though I don't know what kind of life that could have been, since somehow in my mind they ceased to exist from that point on. It never occurred to me that they might still be living and breathing and that I could probably meet them if I wanted to.

I think it is that idea—that my birth parents no longer existed—that more than anything kept me from ever seriously considering looking for them. I used to tell people that I was just afraid of what I might find, but I think the truth is that there just wasn't anyone in my mind's eye to look for. The reality of "birth parents" was so far from my consciousness that I might as well have considered looking for Santa Claus. Heck, at least I could imagine what Santa Claus looked like.

My parents (my adoptive parents, that is) were (and still are) *my parents*. End of story. The birth of my daughter in 2004 did give me pause to reconsider this line of thinking. I could suddenly and overwhelmingly appreciate the enormity of giving birth to a child and immediately handing it over to someone else, expecting to never see it again. And I could not bear the thought of it. When we struggled to conceive a second child, and considered adoption, I shied away from the idea, afraid of coming so close to what I now appreciated to be an extremely emotionally charged experience.

As strange as it sounds, I, an adopted child of loving parents, who knew so much love growing up, wondered if I could love a child that was not my own as much as I loved the daughter that I already had. I'm still puzzled by that doubt.

It was actually my mom that started hinting that I might reach out in some noncommittal way to my birth mother. She dearly wanted that person, if she was still out there, to know that I was okay. Better than okay—that I was healthy, happy, successful . . . all the things a mother might wish for her child. Soon after my daughter was born, Mom asked if I would mind if she wrote a letter to the woman—my birth mother—to place in my file at the Children's Home Society; a letter that she might find if she went looking, but that would not open the file or otherwise divulge who I was. Fine with me, I said.

But when I read her letter, I was overcome with a need for it to be in my own words. Don't send this, I asked her. I wanted to tell her about me myself. But where would I start? How could I possibly begin to edit thirty-seven years of a life down to a page or two to share with the person who gave me life? Short of pondering that impossibility several times, I never did. It was just too overwhelming. How to write a letter to a ghost? I drafted an opening paragraph at least a hundred times in my head, but never wrote a single word.

It's hard for me to remember the exact words that were spoken in that first phone call. I can definitely remember my heart jumping out of my chest, and the sound of the blood rushing through my head. And how easy it was. We just told each other about ourselves; where we had lived and what we did and had done for work and for fun, and whatever we thought the other would want to know about and hear that would reassure her that it had been the right decision. And the more we talked, the more that much seemed clear: Giving me up for adoption at that time in her life allowed us both to have a better life than we would have likely had together. Of course, I had always assumed that anyway, knowing, as I thought I did, that she was too young to be a mother when she had me, and knowing what a great life I had been given.

But I suspected that, for her, knowing that she had been able to live a better life by giving me up might have been little consolation for the guilt connected with the possibility that *my* life had not been so good. I deeply wanted her to know that there was only compassion and understanding for what she did, really had to do, at age fifteen . . . and none of the feelings of longing, abandonment, and resentment that are so often assumed to be felt by adoptees.

So, we had a very thoughtful and gratifying first conversation. I was in graduate school at the time and had to go to class, or we might have just talked through the whole afternoon. We agreed to talk some more that evening, and did. And then it was the weekend, and Ann, Abigail, and I left town as planned to drive down to California. We saw a lot of old friends that weekend, and talking to Shari was all I could talk about. It was all I could think about.

During one of our conversations, I mentioned that Ann and I had been talking about making a trip up to Vancouver Island later in the summer; maybe we could come and meet her instead? Sure, of course, that would be great . . . let's plan on it, we agreed. But by the end of that first weekend, the thought of waiting another month to meet her was unbearable. I called Shari from the road on the way home from California. I had remembered, after snooping around on her website, that she would be playing at a folk festival the next weekend in some place called Canmore. I had no idea where that was . . . but could I come with her? Without a moment's hesitation she answered yes, of course, let me start researching the available flights and we'll talk again when you get home. I said I could afford the flight to Vancouver. She said she would pick up the flight to Calgary. And it was done. It was like that all along as we got to know each other. There was a freedom and an honesty in our communication that is usually only possible with those who have spent a lifetime together. What was especially refreshing about it was that it seemed simply due to the fact that we both preferred our communication that way, and had suddenly found in each other a person who was wired the same way. It wasn't so much that we had maintained some unseen cosmic connection all our lives . . . but just that we saw the world and interacted with the world in very similar ways, and so we felt instantly familiar to one another.

It's difficult for me to fully describe the feeling of validation and reassurance that came from that, except that it gave me an extreme jolt of self-confidence. I mean, here was this woman in the BC Entertainment Hall of Fame, an accomplished musician, with albums and Juno Awards, and . . . she's just like me!

That first flight to Vancouver to meet Shari was the longest day of my life. All day long, and as I paced the terminal in Seattle during an excruciatingly long layover, I kept imagining what all these other people rushing past me might be thinking about. Was it possible that I was the only one in this airport who was flying to meet his birth mother for the first time? Could any of them imagine how crazy that was? I mean, sure, maybe they had important events waiting for them at the other end of their journeys, perhaps a wedding, or a business meeting, or even a funeral, but could any of them possibly top meeting one's birth mother for the first time?

My birth mother!

For the first time!

I didn't dare strike up a conversation with anyone on the airplane for fear that they would ask me where I was going, and was I visiting someone, and how could I possibly tell them the truth, and how could I not? How could I not yell it out to the whole cabin! No, I just kept my nose in my book, my iPod in my ears, and tried not to imagine my head exploding from the anticipation. I swear the customs line, which I had not anticipated, having never flown to Canada before, had been made artificially long just to torture me. The customs agents had clearly been notified of my arrival, and of the reason for my visit, and had all gone on break just to test me and see if I could take the pressure. I'm sure they could all see me sweating from their break room.

After another lifetime waiting for my turn at the counter, the agent asks me the usual questions, all the while staring at his magic computer screen: "Are you visiting?"

"Yes."

"What parts?"

"Bowen Island and Calgary."

"For how long?"

"A week."

"And who are you visiting?"

I pause as I ponder what I am about to say. Finally, "My mother."

"Have you visited her before?"

"No." He pauses as he ponders what I have just said, still staring at his computer screen. "Why not?"

"Because I just met her a week ago."

Silence. He looks at me, taking his eyes off the screen for the first time, with a confused expression, and just nods his head in the direction of the exit. I felt sorry for him. His job did not afford him the freedom to share in what was obviously (to my way of thinking) the most amazing thing that had happened to anyone he would talk to that day.

I was meeting my birth mother!

Then the luggage carousel, then another long hallway, then the person collecting the declaration form, wherever the hell I put that. Oh, for Christ's sake! Am I ever going to get out of this godforsaken airport? I can't keep it together much longer!

Then there it is . . . the exit . . . the place where everyone is waiting. Scanning the room . . . I can't even remember what she looks like anymore . . . my head is swimming . . . I'm not really seeing anything very clearly . . . will she know me?

And there she is. It's her. I drop my bags, and hold out my arms, with a smile so big my face hurts, and I'm hugging her. She's hugging me. I'm thinking, "Does anyone in this room realize what this is? This is me, and my birth mother . . . meeting each other for the first time!" And while I can't overemphasize the joy at finally meeting Shari and standing there in person looking at her, I would be gravely remiss if I didn't mention that I met her daughter, my half-sister, as well, that day, and knew then that I had really hit the jackpot.

I can't remember now how much we had talked about Julia up to that point, but her sweet and gentle nature was apparent from that first meeting. It only added to the relief I felt at that moment, to finally meet them both, and to my excitement as my brain struggled to grasp the possibilities for our relationship that lay ahead.

After a couple of days at her home, meeting friends, lots of friends, everyone who could come and meet the long-lost son, and feeling like a celebrity, we set out for Canmore. Canmore is a beautifully scenic small town in the Rocky Mountains, west of Calgary, that hosts a popular folk music festival every summer. Shari would be playing there with a group called UHF, consisting of her, Bill Henderson, and Roy Forbes. I was a little self-conscious and felt a bit like I was crashing their gig, but they were welcoming, and I just went with the program.

I know it sounds cliché to say, but the whole weekend was truly a once-in-a-lifetime experience. Shari had arranged for me to have my own room at the motel, but by the time we got there, we had been talking non-stop for three days. We heard the price for the extra room, and discovered that her room had an extra fold-out bed in it, and it just made sense to share a room, save the money, and have just that much more time to yak. So we did. By day, I hung around with her and all the musicians that were playing the festival, many of them legends in the Canadian folk music world, but virtually unknown where I lived. Shari announced her discovery and my presence to the crowd at her first turn on the stage, and from that point on, I was treated like visiting royalty by everyone—musicians, fans, and perfect strangers alike.

By night, we would retreat back to the motel and just talk; about the day, about the week, and about our lives. We would talk until four in the morning, the stories becoming increasingly more personal and confessional as it grew later and later. Two to three hours of sleep, and we would be up again, back to the festival, and basking in the glow of the whole experience. Of course, I could lie in the grass and have the occasional snooze while Shari was busy . . . I don't know how she made it through that weekend on so little sleep.

Seeing her play on stage was very moving. People up close to the stage would notice me and wave me over to sit with them so I would have the best view of my new-found birth mother. I remember sitting through one entire set next to a woman I had never met before, who, after introducing me to all her friends, held my hand the entire time . . . just overcome with the emotion of the whole thing.

That weekend at Canmore was like one huge celebration

of our reunion. Of course, we had to come home eventually, first us to Bowen Island for a couple of more days, then me to Eugene. My wife and daughter and I travelled back up a month later and spent a week at Shari's. At the end of that visit, we all travelled together back to Portland for a family reunion, where I met sisters and brothers and nephews and cousins and fathers and wives and felt by then like I had known Shari and Julia for years.

It was suddenly impossible to imagine my life without them in it. My family—my wife, my sister, and especially my mother—were blessedly patient and indulgent with me that first year. Shari and I emailed each other, well, almost every day, or at least it seems like that, looking back on it. If I wasn't talking with her I was talking about her, and I know that it especially left my mother feeling a bit second-rate for a while. But as we have all settled into our new-found roles, or rediscovered the security and permanence of our old ones, it has all just become part of life.

Shari and my mom (and really, she will always be My Mom) quickly forged their own relationship. Rather than becoming some kind of replacement or stand in for a role that was already filled, Shari has become something different in my life; not really a parent, with all the assumptions of responsibility that entails, and much more than a friend. I feel a surprising and strange sense of security in knowing her . . . in knowing she's okay . . . and knowing she knows I'm okay. And though I would have considered myself as someone who could not have felt more loved, the feeling of being loved even more is still overwhelming in a good way.

Forty years seems like an excruciatingly long time to finally solve a mystery like this. But only after having a child of my own could I truly and finally appreciate and understand the complete, enveloping, unconditional love one feels for one's child . . . which in turn allowed me to feel it anew for my parents . . . which finally left my heart perfectly prepared to accept Shari, and all that meeting a birth mother represented; and allowing into my life one who had previously been only a ghost.

Since that first year, the relationship has evolved and continues to evolve. And that's the real beauty of it; that it is now free to become whatever either of us wants and needs it to be. It has become a relationship that fills many of the spaces in between the other, more traditional relationships in our lives: mothers, grandmothers, wives, friends. It is a little bit of all of those, in interesting combinations, and sometimes something else entirely, all at the same time. Rather than replace, it supplements. Shari and Julia expose my daughter to music in a real and personal way that she would not have experienced otherwise. Even I have had the chance to play with them and express musical talents that I had written off after high school.

Though we have all come back down to earth since that first meeting, I feel a sense of having changed inside in a very visceral and positive way. That is something I could never have imagined.

Zahava, Diane, and Jeremy.

Jeremy and Zahava

With a bit of trepidation, I told my children about my project. To my knowledge, neither of them had made any attempt to find their biological families, but we had not really discussed it. I began by asking my son, Jeremy, if he had any interest in searching and if he had questions for me. I had, deep in my dresser drawer, a "brown envelope"—which I now know is common to most adoptive parents!—but had not yet offered to share the contents with either child. I was waiting until they came to me, somehow hoping that they wouldn't.

Although everything I had read and heard indicated that there would be no danger to our relationship or to my "position" as mom, I admit to some deep, dark feelings of anxiety and fear. My fear was partly for me, but even more for Jeremy and Zahava. How would they handle anything they might find? How would they deal with difficult or potentially unpleasant or unwanted relationships?

Jeremy answered quickly and without hesitation. He and I had a good conversation and I gave him his brown envelope. He said he would like to write something for this book and I told him I'd be happy to include it.

Zahava also told me she was curious about her background, and although I didn't have the envelope handy (I had put it away for safekeeping), I told her what I could remember, and she seemed content with that, at least for the time being. To my surprise, she, too, volunteered to write something for this book.

So, although my own children do not actually fit the criteria for the subjects in this book—not having sought, or been found by, their biological families, I am including their stories here. This book is my gift to them and I hope it will answer some of their own questions or raise some issues that they can ponder in their decisions about whether to embark on their own searches.

Jeremy's Story

I was born in Scarborough, a historically rough suburb just east of Toronto. My biological mother was a mixed-race Jewish woman, and my biological father was black and apparently Christian. I know very little about my biological history but that is something I am fine with. Many are surprised to hear that, but let me explain why.

When I was just under a year old, my life changed forever. That was when I was adopted by my two wonderful parents: Diane Koven and Avi Poriah. To this day I think back at how brave they must have been to not only adopt a child, but one who was black, into a family of two white parents. I know that in 2012 this would still make some people uneasy, so I can only imagine what people must have thought in the early '80s.

I grew up in an area called Barrhaven, which is a middle-class, mostly white suburb of Ottawa. People ask me how it was growing up black and Jewish with white parents. The funny thing is, to me, it was never much of an issue. I knew that I was black, and my parents weren't, but in my heart I knew the love we had for one another and I didn't see how it was different than anyone else's relationship with their parents.

Sure, there were some awkward moments here and there. After all, I'm not only black, but also a member of a religion where 99 percent of its members (at least in this part of the world) are white. Not only did my mother and I confuse people when I introduced her as my mother, but Jewish people often were left wondering, "How the heck is this guy Jewish?"

When I was young, I used to ask my mother for a sister. I asked her over and over, and she would brush it off; after all, it's not like you can just pull a sister out of the air — or can you? Before my third birthday, like every other child, I was asked what I wanted for my birthday. My reply: "A baby sister." The day arrived, and I had two little friends over for a birthday lunch. While we were sitting at the table eating my birthday cake, the phone rang. To this day, I don't know who the caller was, but the message my mother received was that a baby girl had been born in a city in New Brunswick and if my parents would like to adopt her, they would have to go right away to take her home from the hospital. When I heard about this, my eyes instantly lit up, as I had got my birthday wish: a baby sister!

Perhaps the way that Zahava came to be my sister accounts for the fact that we have always been very close. In fact, I don't know of any siblings, adopted or not, who are as close as we are. Born of different parents, from different backgrounds, different colours, yet siblings without any doubt.

When we were young, I used to have Zahava speak on my behalf anytime we would go out somewhere public like a shopping mall. Imagine what the store owners would think when they saw me—a big, black kid, and my sister, this small, slim, blonde-haired, blue-eyed girl—and Zahava is doing the talking because I am too shy! I always took the "big brother" role very seriously, and did everything I could to help Zahava grow up, and always felt safe and loved.

Things weren't always perfect. When I was nine years old, my father left us, and my parents were divorced. My mother had to feed two children with very little money. For many, this would be too much to handle, and they would throw in the towel. Not my mother! Not only did she feed and clothe us, but she ensured that we finished our private Jewish education, and also ensured that we went to summer camp each summer and had everything we needed. To this day, I am still not sure how she did it, but somehow, my mother did do it! She made personal sacrifices, took on extra writing jobs, and did whatever it took to ensure that my sister and I had everything we needed. I will be forever grateful to Diane for the selflessness that she showed in raising us, as it's those sacrifices that allowed Zahava and me to develop into the people we are today.

Having lived on this earth for twenty-eight years and having met a lot of people, both adopted and not, I realize just about everyone has issues of some sort. With that said, I feel that my success and stability has everything to do with my mother, her family, and the decisions she made in raising us.

When I was only three years old, I went to a private Jewish day school, beginning in nursery school, and remaining there until graduation from grade eight. There, I met a number of my best friends who to this day I still hang out with, spend time with. When I was ten years old, I went to a summer camp called Camp Kadimah, where I formed close friendships, and in the end found my future business partners, best friends, and my future wife, Aviva.

My mother's family has always been very close to me, treated me with an abundance of love, and helped teach me some vital family values. My grandparents were married for over sixty years, and all of my mother's siblings are still close to this day. My aunts and uncles and cousins love to get together at family occasions. You see a lot of families, adopted or not, who aren't very fond of each other, and I always find that very sad.

Another question I am frequently asked is, "Have you met your biological parents?" and "Why not? Don't you want to know?" For me, my interest in doing so has always been low to moderate at best. While it is interesting knowing certain things about your background I don't see how that changes anything. Clearly my biological mother decided to put me up for adoption. To me, the reason is not important; what is important is that I was so lucky to find a wonderful family who took a young black boy from Scarborough and showed him all the great things the world has to offer.

I think a big reason for my not feeling the need to know can be attributed to where I am in my life. I don't say this to gloat, but I truthfully just want you to understand my thought process.

I am now twenty-eight years old and very happy with my life. I have a wonderful family, I have a sister, Zahava, whom I am very close with. I own a successful business, and I have an amazing and patient girlfriend in Aviva, who one day soon will be my wife.

I feel happy, I feel fulfilled, and I feel like I have everything a man needs. Would it be nice to know what Caribbean island I am from so I could answer when I am asked? Sure. Would it be interesting to meet someone who looks like me? Sure. But at the end of the day, all that means very little to me. What does mean A LOT to me is that Diane Koven and Avi Poriah made the decision to bring me into their life and to raise me into the man that I am today. They are my parents: Diane is my mother; Avi is my father.

Nothing will change that, and even meeting the person who gave birth to me is something I have little interest in. After all, to me, a mother doesn't mean that you simply gave birth to someone. A mother, to me, is someone who raises you, who is there for you throughout your upbringing, and who will sacrifice anything for your happiness. And that is exactly who my mother is: Diane Koven.

Zahava's Story

I'm not sure if the word "luck" is strong enough to describe how fortunate one can be, to have a wonderful family that can love you from birth and form an immediate bond with you without having that blood connection. The first half of my life was always filled with unanswered questions and sometimes uncomfortable situations. After many different scenarios and conversations, I've recently come to realize that focusing on what could have been doesn't really matter, as long as we have the love of our families and friends, and what's most important around us to help us grow and shape ourselves. I have been fortunate enough to have a loving family and people around me that constantly care for me and respect me and my accomplishments.

Some might not understand how difficult it is to feel like a member of a minority, but even the smallest situation to one person can be overwhelming to another. I have always been sensitive to details such as looking like my family members and having the same character traits or interests in common, but I now realize that those things are not what form a family bond.

I was recently visiting home for a weekend with my family, surrounded by loved ones. I gathered the courage to ask about my adoption story. I was told that my birth was unexpected, and a search for a warm, loving home for me had to be conducted in a matter of days. At this time, my brother's birthday happened to be within days of my birth, and he had been requesting a baby sister. I believe it was our predetermined destiny to become a family, based on a series of very fortunate events for everyone involved.

Perhaps the word luck *is* strong enough to describe my unique story, as I now know my past and can move forward with my future. Being lucky is really just being connected by some sort of force that can shape the circumstances, events, and opportunities in our lives. I feel that a chapter in my life has been completed, and with luck on my side, I know I can only move forward and improve my life. I am so proud to be a part of my family; I owe my life to them and am grateful to have been touched by the luck of fate.

AFTERWORD

From the time I began the research for this book, whenever I mentioned it to anyone, I was asked what gave me the idea to write it. How did it come about? Well, there are two answers to that: the answer to how and why I actually decided to write such a book; and the answer to why I had, for as long as I can remember, always been intrigued by the notion of nature vs. nurture. For that's really what this is all about—the question of whether genetics or environment is more important in forming a person's personality and sense of self.

I'll answer the second question first. For what I have always thought was "some unknown reason," I have always felt that I would someday like to adopt a child or children. I also imagined that I would one day be the mother of several biological children and that we would all be one big, happy family. When, in university, I met the man who would become my husband (and later my ex-husband), I was happy to learn that he, too, wanted a big family and wanted to adopt children.

Once we had married, and after twelve years of marriage no biological children had appeared, we did become the adoptive parents of two children. I then had the opportunity to observe up close and first-hand how these children would develop. They came from different biological families; my son is also mixed-race; and they would be growing up as siblings in the same home. I noticed right away, as all parents probably do, that even as babies, these children had certain character traits of their own.

There can never really be a control group for any academic or scientific study of this question. The closest thing to a control group would be a study of identical twins separated at birth and brought up in different environments, but even that is not a true, 100-percent control group. I've read about such experiments, though, and watched a number of fascinating television documentaries showing how these identical twins have amazingly similar characteristics. One study I read claimed that a couple of twins who didn't even know that each other had existed had almost identical likes and dislikes—even to choosing the very same shampoo.

My completely unscientific "study" of the question, using my own children as subjects, has brought me to the conclusion that everyone is born with certain character traits, but one's environment will serve to either encourage and nurture, or squelch such traits. For example, I am a very sociable person. I love to have people around, have always had many friends, and participate in a variety of activities. I love to laugh and have a good time. Both of my children, coming from completely different biological backgrounds, are also very sociable, "people" people who have strong, long-time friendships; and both have a great sense of humour. I feel sure that this is the result of growing up in such an environment.

So, even though I have my own theories about how one's identity is shaped, I often wondered how adoptees felt about it. I wonder how I would feel if I had been adopted. Would I feel that I were living a "pretend" life and wonder who I would have been—who I was "meant" to be? Was this a question that most adoptees had? More to the point, did my own children wonder, and would they feel a need to search for their biological roots?

As to the question about why I decided to write this book, I could say it was an epiphany. I have been a writer since I was able to write, quite literally. I can recall as a very young child, perhaps in Grade 2 or 3, pounding away on an old typewriter at my grandparents' house, writing a "newspaper" of family news, jokes I "borrowed" from a book of jokes on their bookshelf, gossip, etc. I had to retype each copy (way before word processors or computers!) and I sold each one for five cents!

In university, though I majored in English, I took journalism courses and later got a media communications diploma from a community college. I did occasional freelance writing and broadcasting but for some reason did not pursue this as my full-time career.

Over the years, my freelance writing increased—for magazines, local newspapers, corporate newsletters, brochures, and so forth. In the back of my mind, I always hoped that someday I would write a book. I think every writer harbours that dream. There are writers in my family: My mother published a book, then my cousin, then my sister-in-law. I belonged to a writers' critique group where I read my stories in progress, usually human interest, "people stories," which is my specialty.

At one meeting, one of the members asked me when I was going to write a book. I replied that I had just come to the conclusion that I wouldn't write one; that I couldn't write one. "Why not?" she asked. Well, I had realized that I just don't have a good enough imagination to write a book. "You don't have to write fiction," she said. "You have lots of stories. You're a good writer. Write about what you know."

I thanked her for her kind words, but really didn't think I had anything worthwhile to write about. I stopped attending the critique group, continued to write my 500-word articles, and more or less forgot about my dream of writing a book.

Then, one day, I went to the golf course for my weekly game with a women's league (my love-hate—mostly hate—relationship with golf could be the subject of another book!). It started to rain just as I arrived and parked my car. I ran to the clubhouse, thinking it might stop. Instead, the rain became torrential, and there was no sign of its abating anytime soon. Three other women standing nearby decided that since they were there and had blocked off the time anyway, they would go into the clubhouse for a drink; they asked if I'd like to join them. That could have been one of the best drinks I've ever had, because it led directly to this book.

One of the women was telling the other two (they worked together and were friends as well) that after her mother had recently died, she was cleaning out her apartment, and in a dresser drawer came across a large, brown envelope. Looking inside, she found documents about her adoption. The woman had always known she was adopted but knew almost nothing about her background, and her parents had never discussed it with her. She had a warm and loving relationship with her parents and had never felt the need to know about her biological family. She also feared that if she had asked any questions, she would have upset her parents—which she definitely didn't want to do.

The conversation ensued, with one of the other women joining in to tell the others that her husband, a middle-aged dairy farmer, had been reunited with his biological mother the year before. With adoption stories swirling around me, I was fascinated to hear the details. I mentioned that my own two children were adopted and instantly bonded with the others.

When I went home that night, I couldn't sleep. I felt "wound up," and thoughts were spinning through my head all night. At one point during the night, I really felt like a light bulb had been turned on—I had the idea for my book! It was the perfect melding of all the areas of my life—my love of writing, my love of human interest stories, my fascination with adoption and how it shapes a person. I even "saw" the title—*Who Am I, Really?*—in my head.

I was so excited that I could think of nothing else for the next few days. I jotted down ideas, notes, questions. The following week when I went to the golf course, I eagerly sought out the other women and told them of my idea. I asked if they would be willing to participate. They were both immediately enthusiastic about the idea and the title of the book. They gave me their contact information. One woman said she'd speak to her husband (who also agreed immediately to be interviewed), and my book was born.

ABOUT THE AUTHOR

Diane Koven is a Certified Financial Planner, Certified Health Specialist, and Certified Divorce Financial Analyst with Sunlife Financial in Ottawa, Ontario. She is a graduate of Carleton University (English Literature) and Algonquin College (Media Communications) and has been a freelance writer for over three decades. She is an avid Nordic walker, has participated in several Dragon Boat races, and enjoys watercolour painting and new adventures. The most rewarding experience of her life continues to be her role of mother to two exceptionally wonderful children.

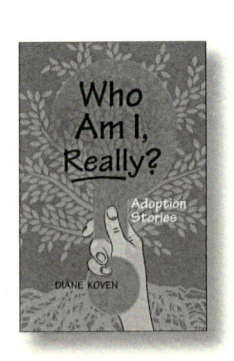

TO ORDER MORE COPIES:

GSPH

GENERAL STORE PUBLISHING HOUSE INC.
499 O'Brien Road, Box 415, Renfrew, Ontario, Canada K7V 4A6
Tel 1.800.465.6072 • Fax 1.613.432.7184
www.gsph.com

VISA MasterCard